English Langu

Station Activities

for Common Core State Standards

Grades 6–8

Susan Brooks-Young

WALCH EDUCATION®

1   2   3   4   5   6   7   8   9   10

ISBN 978-0-8251-6873-4

Copyright © 2011

J. Weston Walch, Publisher

40 Walch Drive • Portland, ME 04103

www.walch.com

Printed in the United States of America

Table of Contents

English Language Arts Station Activities for Common Core State Standards

Introduction

This book includes a collection of station-based activities to provide students with opportunities to practice and apply the skills and concepts they learn in class. It contains station activities for each of the following Common Core Standards for middle school English Language Arts: Reading—Literature; Reading—Informational Text; Writing; and Language. Speaking and Listening standards are infused throughout the station activities.

- The Reading activities explore text complexity and comprehension.
- The Writing activities cover specific types of writing, response to reading, and research.
- The Language activities provide practice with English language usage and conventions.

Use these activities in addition to direct instruction lessons or instead of direct instruction in areas where students grasp the basic concepts but need practice. The debriefing discussions after each set of activities provide an important opportunity to help students reflect on their experiences and synthesize their thinking. They also provide an additional opportunity for ongoing, informal assessment to inform instructional planning.

Implementation Guide

The following guidelines will help you prepare for and use the activity sets in this section.

Setting Up the Stations

Each activity set consists of four stations. Set up each station at a desk, or at several desks pushed together, with enough chairs for a small group of students. Place a card with the number of the station on the desk. Each station should also contain the materials specified in the teacher's notes and a stack of student activity sheets (one copy per student in the class). Place the required materials (as listed) at each station.

When a group of students arrives at a station, each student should take one of the activity sheets to record the group's work. Although students should work together to develop one set of answers for the entire group, each student should record the answers on his or her own activity sheet. This helps keep students engaged in the activity and gives each student a record of the activity for future reference.

Forming Groups of Students

The activity sets consist of four stations. You might divide the class into four groups by having students count off from 1 to 4. If you have a large class and want to have students working in small groups, you might set up two identical sets of stations, labeled A and B. In this way, the class can be divided into eight groups, with each group of students rotating through the A stations or the B stations.

Assigning Roles to Students

Students often work most productively in groups when each student has an assigned role. You may want to assign roles to students when they are assigned to groups and change the roles occasionally. Some possible roles are as follows:

- Reader—reads the steps of the activity aloud
- Facilitator—makes sure that each member of the group has a chance to speak and pose questions; also makes sure that each student agrees on each answer before it is written down
- Materials Manager—handles the materials at the station and makes sure the materials are put back in place at the end of the activity
- Timekeeper—tracks the group's progress to ensure that the activity is completed in the allotted time
- Spokesperson—speaks for the group during the debriefing session after the activities

Timing the Activities

The activities in each section are designed to take approximately 20 minutes per station. Therefore, you might plan on having groups change stations every 20 minutes, with a 2-minute interval for moving from one station to the next. It is helpful to give students a "5-minute warning" before it is time to change stations.

Since the activity sets consist of four stations, the above time frame means that it will take about 1 hour and 30 minutes for groups to work through all stations. If this is followed by a 20-minute class discussion as described below, an entire activity set can be completed in about 2 hours.

Introduction

Guidelines for Students

Before starting the first activity set, you may want to review the following "ground rules" with students. You might also post the rules in the classroom.

- All students in a group should agree on each answer before it is written down. If there is a disagreement within the group, discuss it with one another.
- You can ask the teacher a question only if everyone in the group has the same question.
- If you finish early, work together to write problems of your own that are similar to the ones on the student activity sheet.
- Leave the station exactly as you found it. All materials should be in the same place and in the same condition as when you arrived.

Debriefing the Activities

After all groups have rotated through all stations, bring students together for a brief class discussion. At this time, you might have the groups' spokespersons pose any questions they had about the activities. Before responding, ask if students in other groups encountered the same difficulty or if they have a response to the question. The class discussion is also a good time to draw out the essential ideas of the activities. The questions that are provided in the teacher's notes for each activity set can serve as a guide to initiating this type of discussion.

You may want to collect the student activity sheets before beginning the class discussion. However, it can be beneficial to collect the sheets afterward so that students can refer to them during the discussion. This also gives students a chance to revisit and refine their work based on the debriefing session.

Guide to Common Core Standards Annotation

As you use this book, you will come across standards annotated with an asterisk (*) for several station activity sets. According to the Common Core State Standards Initiative Web site, at www.corestandards.org, "Skills and understandings that are particularly likely to require continued attention in higher grades as they are applied to increasingly sophisticated writing and speaking are marked with an asterisk (*)."

Materials List

Class Sets

- grade level reading material (may include novels, textbooks, newspaper or magazine articles, etc.)
- highlighters (including four each of yellow, pink, and blue)

Ongoing Use

- drawing paper
- notebook paper
- pens or pencils

Station Sets

- two poems with a central theme for each student (The poems may come from a textbook, anthology, or online collection such as the Theme Poem Collection: http://poetry.about.com/od/ourpoemcollections/Theme_Poem_Collections_The_About_Poetry_Anthologies.htm.)
- three short newspaper or magazine articles (1 page or less)
- four or five pictures of common symbols (e.g., a bald eagle to represent the U.S. government)
- four red pencils (one per student at the station)
- six to eight index cards
- a short passage from a story that uses imagery to describe characters, setting, and/or action
- access to computers and the Internet
- assorted reference materials (include at least one each of the following: book; encyclopedia volume; magazine, newspaper, or journal article; video or film; printout of Web site home page)
- colored markers (red, blue, yellow, green—one set per group member)
- copies of a photograph with no caption
- copies of a short narrative poem such as Robert Frost's "The Road Not Taken"
- copies of blank plot map (reproducible from page 15)

Materials List

Station Sets (*continued*)

- Newspapers will be specifically required in several activities. The following materials need to come from newspapers:
    - two newspaper articles (from different sources) that address the same topic
    - three print advertisements that use hyperbole
    - a newspaper article about a local event or topic
    - a printed advertisement
    - a Sunday comic strip that tells a self-contained story (not a serial strip)
    - editorials/opinion pieces
    - the front section of a newspaper
- student writing samples of the following types (with identifying information removed):
    - sample that includes few or no details
    - sample that needs to be rearranged for clarity
    - sample that includes too many details or unrelated information
    - sample that includes text that needs to be replaced for clarity
    - two to three short samples of each student's own writing from past assignments

Reading—Literature

Set 1: Pre-Reading Strategies

Goal: To provide opportunities for students to develop concepts and skills related to use of pre-reading strategies in order to increase comprehension and accurate interpretation of text

Common Core Standards, Grade 6

Reading—Literature: Key Ideas and Details

RL.6.1. Cite textual evidence to support analysis of what the text says explicitly as well as inferences drawn from the text.

RL.6.2. Determine a theme or central idea of a text and how it is conveyed through particular details....

Common Core Standards, Grade 7

Reading—Literature: Key Ideas and Details

RL.7.1. Cite several pieces of textual evidence to support analysis of what the text says explicitly as well as inferences drawn from the text.

Common Core Standards, Grade 8

Reading—Literature: Key Ideas and Details

RL.8.1. Cite the textual evidence that most strongly supports an analysis of what the text says explicitly as well as inferences drawn from the text.

Student Activities Overview and Answer Key

Station 1

Students work together to preview the content and organization of an assigned reading.

Answers

Answers will vary depending upon the assigned text. Accept any reasonable responses.

Station 2

Students make predictions to answer questions and then make predictions about an assigned reading.

Answers

1. Mexican food
2. someone who is 6' tall
3. *A Midsummer Night's Dream*

Accept any reasonable predictions made about the assigned reading.

Station 3

Students work together to identify the topic of an assigned reading and chart their prior knowledge about the topic.

Answers

Answers will vary depending upon the assigned text. Accept any reasonable responses.

Station 4

Students establish a purpose for reading an assigned text by formulating questions about what they hope to learn and why this information might be important.

Answers

Answers will vary depending upon the assigned text. Accept any reasonable responses.

Materials List/Setup

Note: By using the same reading selection at each station, students will progress through all four recommended pre-reading strategies. You may want to repeat these stations whenever the class reads a new selection or until students master and use the pre-reading strategies on their own. However, you may also use different reading selections at each station.

Station 1 reading material, one copy per student (may include a novel, textbook, article, etc.)

Station 2 reading material, one copy per student (may include a novel, textbook, article, etc.)

Station 3 reading material, one copy per student (may include a novel, textbook, article, etc.)

Station 4 reading material, one copy per student (may include a novel, textbook, article, etc.)

Discussion Guide

To support students in reflecting on the activities and to gather some formative information about student learning, use the following prompts to facilitate a class discussion to "debrief" the station activities.

Prompts/Questions

1. Describe what you learn about a text by previewing it.

2. Compare previewing a text and making predictions about a text.

3. Describe three ways you can connect a new text to your prior knowledge about a topic.

4. Discuss how writing purpose questions can help you understand a text.

Think, Pair, Share

Have students jot down their own responses to questions, then discuss with a partner (who was not in their station group), and then discuss as a whole class.

Suggested Appropriate Responses

1. Previewing a text prepares a reader for what he or she is about to read, providing clues about the content and structure of the material.

2. When you preview a text, you get a sense of what you'll be reading, based upon the content and structure of the text. When you make predictions, you use clues to get an idea of what the text is about.

3. You can tap into prior knowledge by thinking about other texts you've read on the same topic or written by the same author; by making connections to your own personal experience; or by making connections to an example of a real-world situation.

4. Asking questions about a text before reading helps you focus on the meaning of the material while you read.

Possible Misunderstandings/Mistakes

- Forgetting that pre-reading does not require in-depth reading of the text
- Making predictions before completely previewing a text
- Using purpose questions to make predictions

Reading—Literature
Set 1: Pre-Reading Strategies

Station 1: Previewing

You will find an assigned reading at this station. It may be a book, a chapter from a textbook, an article, or other document your teacher assigns. Use this chart to preview the content and organization of the reading. Afterward, compare your work with the work of other members of your group. Add notes to your chart, as needed.

Previewing a Text

Title of text: _____

Items to Review	Your Notes
Text Organization What kind of document are you previewing? How is the text organized? Is there a table of contents? Are there sections? Chapters? What does the text organization tell you about the assigned reading?	
Title and/or Subtitle What information does the title provide about the text? If there are subtitles, what information do they provide?	
Author Is the author named? What is his/her name? Do you recognize this name? What do you know about the author?	

continued

Reading—Literature
Set 1: Pre-Reading Strategies

Items to Review	Your Notes
Publication Date and Publisher When was this text published and by whom? What does this tell you about the content?	
Artwork/Graphics What images are included in the text? What information is provided by these images?	
Main Ideas Read the first and last sentences in several paragraphs. What do these sentences tell you about the text?	

English Language Arts Station Activities for Common Core State Standards

Reading—Literature
Set 1: Pre-Reading Strategies

Station 2: Making Predictions

You will find an assigned reading at this station. It may be a book, a chapter from a textbook, an article, or other document your teacher assigns. Once you've answered the first three questions on this sheet, use the assigned reading to answer the questions on the next page.

When you predict something, you are making an educated guess about what will happen in the future, based upon information you already have. For example, a meteorologist predicts the weather by combining information about current weather conditions and past weather patterns.

Make predictions to answer the following questions.

1. What kind of food would most likely be on the menu at a restaurant named South of the Border?

    _____

2. Who would most likely be a better basketball player—someone who is 5'1" tall, or someone who is 6' tall?

    _____

3. Based on the title, which of these plays is most likely a comedy—*Death of a Salesman* or *A Midsummer Night's Dream?*

    _____

continued

Reading—Literature
Set 1: Pre-Reading Strategies

Look at your assigned reading. Use your predicting skills to answer the following questions.

4. Read the title. What can you predict about the text, based on the title?

_____

_____

_____

_____

5. Look at any artwork/graphics. What can you predict about the text, based on these images? If there are no images, can you predict why?

_____

_____

_____

_____

6. Look at the way the text is organized. Can you make predictions about the text based on its layout?

_____

_____

_____

_____

7. Discuss your predictions with other members of your group. What do you notice?

_____

_____

_____

_____

_____

_____

Reading—Literature
Set 1: Pre-Reading Strategies

Station 3: Using Prior Knowledge

You will find an assigned reading at this station. It may be a book, a chapter from a textbook, an article, or other document your teacher assigns. Work with your group to decide the topic of this reading. Use the chart to identify what you already know about that topic.

Look at the text features that provide clues about the topic of the assigned reading. This may include the title, headings, illustrations, and the first paragraph. Discuss the information you find with your group. Write the topic of the reading below.

_____

_____

Once your Facilitator checks the identified topic with your teacher, each group member should complete the chart below.

Using Prior Knowledge

Title of text: _____

Make a list of other books, articles, or resources you have already seen that were about the same topic and/or written by the same author.	List what you already know about this topic from personal experience.	Describe one or more examples of ways this topic applies to real life.

Reading—Literature
Set 1: Pre-Reading Strategies

Station 4: Reading with Purpose

You will find an assigned reading at this station. It may be a book, a chapter from a textbook, an article, or other document your teacher assigns. Use the chart on the next page to write questions about the reading.

Look at the text features that provide clues about the assigned reading such as the title, headings, illustrations, and the first paragraph. The clues you find will also raise questions about what you can learn from this assigned reading and why this information might be important for you to learn. Write at least one question in each row in the chart on the next page.

After completing the chart, share your questions with your group. Listen to their questions. Do you want to add a new question or change one that you wrote? Take a few minutes to update your chart.

Reading—Literature
Set 1: Pre-Reading Strategies

Reading with Purpose Title of text:	Who?	What?	When?	Where?	Why?	How?

Reading—Literature

Goal: To provide opportunities for students to practice various strategies for increasing reading comprehension, including identifying plot elements, character dimensions, conflict types, and elements of the setting

Common Core Standards, Grade 6

Reading—Literature: Key Ideas and Details

RL.6.1. Cite textual evidence to support analysis of what the text says explicitly as well as inferences drawn from the text.

RL.6.2. Determine a theme or central idea of a text and how it is conveyed through particular details....

RL.6.3. Describe how a particular story's or drama's plot unfolds in a series of episodes as well as how the characters respond or change as the plot moves toward a resolution.

Reading—Literature: Craft and Structure

RL.6.5. Analyze how a particular sentence, chapter, scene, or stanza fits into the overall structure of a text and contributes to the development of the theme, setting, or plot.

Common Core Standards, Grade 7

Reading—Literature: Key Ideas and Details

RL.7.1. Cite several pieces of textual evidence to support analysis of what the text says explicitly as well as inferences drawn from the text.

RL.7.2. Determine a theme or central idea of a text and analyze its development over the course of the text; provide an objective summary of the text.

RL.7.3. Analyze how particular elements of a story or drama interact (e.g., how setting shapes the characters or plot).

Reading—Literature: Craft and Structure

RL.7.6. Analyze how an author develops and contrasts the points of view of different characters or narrators in a text.

Common Core Standards, Grade 8

Reading—Literature: Key Ideas and Details

RL.8.1. Cite the textual evidence that most strongly supports an analysis of what the text says explicitly as well as inferences drawn from the text.

RL.8.2. Determine a theme or central idea of a text and analyze its development over the course of the text, including its relationship to the characters, setting, and plot; provide an objective summary of the text.

RL.8.3. Analyze how particular lines of dialogue or incidents in a story or drama propel the action, reveal aspects of a character, or provoke a decision.

Reading—Literature: Craft and Structure

RL.8.6. Analyze how differences in the points of view of the characters and the audience or reader (e.g., created through the use of dramatic irony) create such effects as suspense or humor.

Student Activities Overview and Answer Key
Station 1

Students identify the four elements of plot in a Sunday comic strip story.

Answers

Answers will vary depending upon the Sunday comic strip selected. Accept any reasonable responses.

Station 2

Students describe three dimensions of a character in a Sunday comic strip story.

Answers

Answers will vary depending upon the Sunday comic strip selected. Accept any reasonable responses.

Station 3

Students identify the type of conflict found in a Sunday comic strip story and write a brief justification for their choice.

Answers

Answers will vary depending upon the Sunday comic strip selected. Accept any reasonable responses.

Station 4

Students identify the setting for a Sunday comic strip story and write a brief justification for their choice.

Answers

Answers will vary depending upon the Sunday comic strip selected. Accept any reasonable responses.

Materials List/Setup

Note: You may use a different Sunday comic strip at each station or use the same strip at each station. Choose a comic strip that tells a self-contained story (not a serial strip).

Station 1 copies of a Sunday comic strip

Station 2 copies of a Sunday comic strip

Station 3 copies of a Sunday comic strip

Station 4 copies of a Sunday comic strip

Discussion Guide

To support students in reflecting on the activities and to gather some formative information about student learning, use the following prompts to facilitate a class discussion to "debrief" the station activities.

Prompts/Questions

1. Discuss the role of each of the four elements of plot in a story.

2. Why is it important to think about all three dimensions of a character?

3. Do you think that a story can include more than one type of conflict? Explain.

4. Why is setting important?

Think, Pair, Share

Have students jot down their own responses to questions, then discuss with a partner (who was not in their station group), and then discuss as a whole class.

Suggested Appropriate Responses

1. A good plot includes elements that support the central conflict. It introduces a core problem through the rising action, has a turning point (climax) and falling action(s), and then brings the story to some kind of resolution.

2. Interesting stories have well-defined characters. Understanding the characters is an important part of understanding the story itself.

3. Yes. There is probably only one major conflict, but stories often have smaller conflicts as well.

4. In a well-written story, setting plays an important role in developing the plot and in how the reader responds to the story.

Possible Misunderstandings/Mistakes

- Thinking that the climax of the story is also the end of the story
- Forgetting to pay close attention to all dimensions of a character
- Forgetting that the setting often provides important clues about the author's purpose

Reading—Literature
Set 2: Story Elements

Station 1: Plot

You will find copies of a Sunday comic strip at this station. You will use the comic strip and this activity sheet to complete the station activity.

The plot of a story is the sum of all the action in the story. A good plot includes four elements:

- **Rising Action:** a series of events that lead to the climax
- **Climax:** turning point of the action
- **Falling Action:** events that occur after the climax
- **Resolution:** the conclusion of the story

Sunday comic strips tell stories that include these elements. Read the comic strip you find at this station and use the chart below to answer the questions and identify the plot elements. Write your answers in the space provided. Compare and discuss your answers with the group.

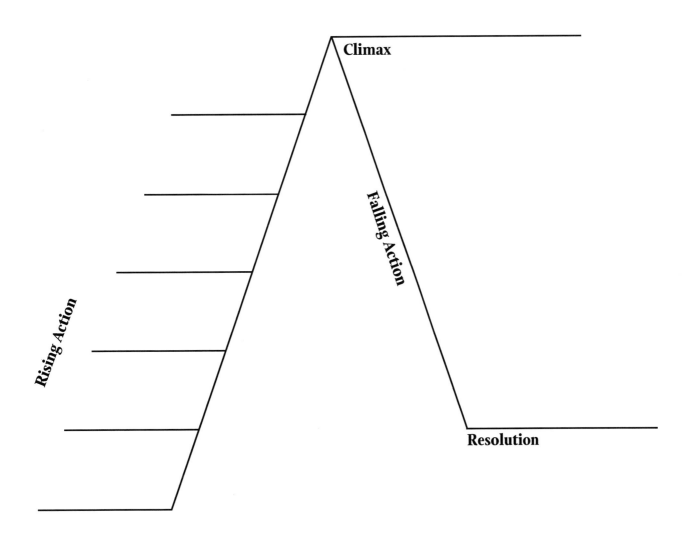

Reading—Literature
Set 2: Story Elements

Station 2: Character

You will find copies of a Sunday comic strip at this station. You will use the comic strip and this activity sheet to complete the station activity.

A **character** is an individual figure in a story. Just as in real life, characters in stories have several dimensions, including:

- **Outer:** a physical description of the character
- **Social:** general and personal relationships with other characters, such as occupation, place in family structure, or friendships
- **Inner:** the emotional and moral characteristics of a character

To tell an interesting story in just a few panels, a comic strip must reveal as much as possible about the characters as quickly as possible, through appearance, relationships, and actions. Read the comic strip. Choose one of the main characters in the story. Write the character's name in the chart below. If the name is not given, write a short description that identifies that character. Then list the information the comic strip provides about the dimensions of that character.

Character Dimensions

Name of character: _____

Outer	Social	Inner

Discuss your chart with your group. Which characters did other group members choose? If someone chose the same character, how are your charts alike and different?

Reading—Literature
Set 2: Story Elements

Station 3: Conflict

You will find copies of a Sunday comic strip at this station. You will use the comic strip and this activity sheet to complete the station activity.

A conflict is the opposition between two forces in a story. One force, usually the main character (protagonist), is up against another force (antagonist). There are four types of conflicts:

- **Person versus Person:** conflict with another character
- **Person versus Nature:** contest between the protagonist and the environment
- **Person versus Society:** struggle with social issues, such as war or poverty
- **Person versus Self:** inner struggle between self and own feelings

1. Read the comic strip at this station. As you read, look for the conflict in the story. Who or what is opposing the main character? When you find the conflict, describe it in the space provided below.

   _____

   _____

2. Review the four types of conflict. Which type of conflict happens in this story? Write your answer on the lines below.

   _____

   _____

   _____

3. What details in the story led you to the answers you wrote above?

   _____

   _____

   _____

4. Share your answers with your group. Did anyone identify a different conflict or a different type of conflict? What reasons did that person give? Do you need to change anything in your answers?

   _____

   _____

Reading—Literature
Set 2: Story Elements

Station 4: Setting

You will find copies of a Sunday comic strip at this station. You will use the comic strip and this activity sheet to complete the station activity.

Setting is the time and place in which actions happen in a story. Setting is important because it influences the way a reader thinks about the events in the story. For example, a character being followed by a stranger on a crowded street in the middle of the day brings a different response from a reader than when the same character is followed by the same stranger in a lonely place during a midnight storm.

1. Look at the comic strip. What is the setting? Where are the characters? Can you tell the time of day? Are there other clues about the tone the cartoonist wants to set, such as weather?

_____

_____

_____

_____

2. What details do you see to support your answer?

_____

_____

_____

_____

3. What mood is the cartoonist trying to establish with this setting?

_____

_____

_____

_____

Reading—Literature

Instruction

Goal: To provide opportunities for students to explore and understand poetry

Common Core Standards, Grade 6

Reading—Literature: Key Ideas and Details

RL.6.1.   Cite textual evidence to support analysis of what the text says explicitly as well as inferences drawn from the text.

RL.6.2.   Determine a theme or central idea of a text and how it is conveyed through particular details; provide a summary of the text distinct from personal opinions or judgments.

RL.6.3.   Describe how a particular story's or drama's plot unfolds in a series of episodes as well as how the characters respond or change as the plot moves toward a resolution.

Reading—Literature: Craft and Structure

RL.6.4.   Determine the meaning of words and phrases as they are used in a text, including figurative and connotative meanings; analyze the impact of a specific word choice on meaning and tone.

RL.6.5.   Analyze how a particular sentence, chapter, scene, or stanza fits into the overall structure of a text and contributes to the development of the theme, setting, or plot.

Common Core Standards, Grade 7

Reading—Literature: Key Ideas and Details

RL.7.1.   Cite several pieces of textual evidence to support analysis of what the text says explicitly as well as inferences drawn from the text.

RL.7.2.   Determine a theme or central idea of a text and analyze its development over the course of the text; provide an objective summary of the text.

Reading—Literature: Craft and Structure

RL.7.4.   Determine the meaning of words and phrases as they are used in a text, including figurative and connotative meanings; analyze the impact of rhymes and other repetitions of sounds (e.g., alliteration) on a specific verse or stanza of a poem or section of a story or drama.

RL.7.5.   Analyze how a drama's or poem's form or structure (e.g., soliloquy, sonnet) contributes to its meaning.

Common Core Standards, Grade 8

Reading—Literature: Key Ideas and Details

RL.8.1.   Cite the textual evidence that most strongly supports an analysis of what the text says explicitly as well as inferences drawn from the text.

RL.8.2.   Determine a theme or central idea of a text and analyze its development over the course of the text, including its relationship to the characters, setting, and plot; provide an objective summary of the text.

Reading—Literature: Craft and Structure

RL.8.4.   Determine the meaning of words and phrases as they are used in a text, including figurative and connotative meanings; analyze the impact of specific word choices on meaning and tone, including analogies or allusions to other texts.

RL.8.5.   Compare and contrast the structure of two or more texts and analyze how the differing structure of each text contributes to its meaning and style.

Student Activities Overview and Answer Key
Station 1

Students identify examples of alliteration in lines from famous poetry and then write a short poem (no more than four lines) that uses alliteration in each line.

Answers

1. cobbles, clattered, clashed

2. sings, solitary, song

3. whistles, wind

Discussion responses will vary.

Station 2

Students identify examples of assonance in lines from famous sayings and poetry and then write a sentence that uses assonance.

Answers

1. ow

2. ai

3. all long i's

4. all long o's

5. long i's in first line, long a's in second line

Station 3

Students identify the four elements of plot in a narrative poem.

Answers

Answers will vary depending upon the narrative poem selected. Accept any reasonable responses.

Station 4

Students practice their skills identifying common themes in two poems.

Answers

Answers will vary. Accept any reasonable responses.

Materials List/Setup

Station 1   none

Station 2   none

Station 3   copies of a short narrative poem (such as Robert Frost's "The Road Not Taken"); copies of blank plot map (can be reproduced from page 15)

Station 4   copies of two poems with a central theme for each student (The poems may come from a textbook, anthology, or online collection such as the Theme Poem Collection: http://poetry.about.com/od/ourpoemcollections/ Theme_Poem_Collections_The_About_Poetry_Anthologies.htm.)

Discussion Guide

To support students in reflecting on the activities and to gather some formative information about student learning, use the following prompts to facilitate a class discussion to "debrief" the station activities.

Prompts/Questions

1. Contrast the differences between alliteration and assonance.

2. Compare the similarities between alliteration and assonance.

3. Discuss how a narrative poem is like a short story.

4. What is the difference between the subject of a poem and the poem's theme?

Think, Pair, Share

Have students jot down their own responses to questions, then discuss with a partner (who was not in their station group), and then discuss as a whole class.

Suggested Appropriate Responses

1. Alliteration is repeated use of initial consonant sounds and assonance is repeated use of vowel sounds. Also, overuse of alliteration makes a poem sound silly, like a tongue twister.

2. Both use letter sounds to enrich the way a poem sounds.

3. Narrative poems include the four elements of plot.

4. The subject of a poem is a general topic such as "death" or "honesty." The theme of a poem tells you the poet's thoughts or feelings about the subject.

Possible Misunderstandings/Mistakes

- Confusing the terms alliteration and assonance
- Not realizing that the narrator of a poem is also a character
- Confusing the terms subject and theme

Reading—Literature
Set 3: Poetry

Station 1: Alliteration

Use the poetry examples on this worksheet to practice your skills at recognizing alliteration.

Repeating the same beginning consonant sound in at least two words in a sentence or line of poetry is called **alliteration**. Read this line from Alfred Noyes's poem, "The Highwayman":

"Over the cobbles he clattered and clashed in the dark innyard."

1. What beginning consonant sound does Noyes repeat three times in this line? Underline the words that begin with the same consonant sound.

Share your answers with your group. Did you all underline the same three words? If not, talk about your answers and see if you can agree on the answers.

Read these lines from William Wordsworth's poem, "Lucy Gray":

"And sings a solitary song
That whistles in the wind."

Wordsworth uses alliteration in both lines, but the repeating beginning consonant sounds are different in each line.

2. What beginning consonant sound is repeated in the first line? Underline the words that begin with that sound.

3. What beginning consonant sound is repeated in the second line? Underline the words that begin with that sound.

Share your answers with your group. Did you all underline the same words? If not, talk about your answers and see if you can agree on the answers.

When a writer overuses alliteration, the text sounds silly. A tongue twister such as "Rubber baby buggy bumpers" is an example. Write a short tongue twister below. Add as much alliteration as you can.

_____

_____

Read your tongue twister to your group. Explain the process you used to write the sentence.

Reading—Literature
Set 3: Poetry

Station 2: Assonance

Use the examples from well-known literature on this worksheet to practice your skills at recognizing assonance.

Repeating the same vowel sound in a series of words is called **assonance**. What vowel sounds are repeated in each of these examples? Underline the letters that make the repeated vowel sounds.

1. How now, brown cow.

2. The rain in Spain falls mainly on the plains.

Share your answers with your group. Did you all underline the same letters in each example? If not, talk about your answers and see if you can agree on the answers.

What vowel sounds are repeated in each of the examples below? Underline the letters that make the repeated vowel sounds.

3. "And so, all the night-tide, I lie down by the side
   Of my darling, my darling, my life and my bride."

   —Edgar Allan Poe, "Annabel Lee"

4. "Poetry is old, ancient, goes back far. It is among the oldest of living things. So old it is that no man knows how and why the first poems came."

   —Carl Sandburg, "Early Moon"

This last example is tricky. The writer uses assonance in both lines, but the repeating vowel sounds are different in each line. Underline the letters that make the repeated vowel sounds in each line.

5. "Night came on, and a full moon rose high over the trees into the sky, lighting the land till it lay bathed in ghostly day."

   —Jack London, The Call of the Wild

Now it's your turn. Use the lines below to write a sentence that includes a series of words that repeat the same vowel sound.

_____

_____

Read your sentence to your group. Explain the process you used to write the sentence.

Reading—Literature
Set 3: Poetry

Station 3: Narrative Poetry

You will find copies of a narrative poem and a blank plot map at this station.

The **plot** of a story is the action in the story. A good plot includes four elements:

- **Rising action:** series of events that lead to the climax
- **Climax:** turning point of the action
- **Falling action:** events that occur after the climax
- **Resolution:** the conclusion of the story

Narrative poems tell stories that include these elements. Read the narrative poem at this station and use the copy of the plot map provided to answer the questions and identify the plot elements. Write your answers in the space provided. Compare and discuss your answers with your group.

Plot Elements

1. What is the basic problem in the story? _____

   _____

2. Who are the characters in the story? _____

   _____

3. Rising action (there will be several events to list here): _____

   _____

   _____

4. Climax: _____

   _____

5. Falling action (there may be several events to list here): _____

   _____

   _____

6. Resolution: _____

   _____

English Language Arts Station Activities for Common Core State Standards

Reading—Literature
Set 3: Poetry

Station 4: Theme

You will find copies of two poems at this station. Use the questions on this activity sheet to identify the common theme for these poems.

The subject of a poem is a general topic such as "death" or "honesty." The theme of a poem tells you the poet's thoughts or feelings about the subject, such as "death comes to everyone" or "honesty is always rewarded." Read the poems and answer the following questions to identify the common theme of these poems.

Poem 1

Write the title here: _____

1. What is the subject of this poem?

   _____

   _____

   _____

2. What clues are given in the poem to help you identify the subject?

   _____

   _____

   _____

3. How does the poet feel about this subject?

   _____

   _____

   _____

   _____

4. What clues in the poem support your answer?

   _____

   _____

   _____

   _____

continued

English Language Arts Station Activities for Common Core State Standards

Reading—Literature
Set 3: Poetry

Poem 2

Write the title here: _____

1. What is the subject of this poem?

   _____

   _____

   _____

2. What clues are given in the poem to help you identify the subject?

   _____

   _____

   _____

3. How does the poet feel about this subject?

   _____

   _____

   _____

   _____

4. What clues in the poem support your answer?

   _____

   _____

   _____

   _____

Poems 1 and 2

What is the common theme for these two poems?

_____

_____

   Share and discuss your answers with members of your group. Did you all identify the same
common theme? How are your answers similar and how are they different?

Reading—Literature

Set 4: Imagery and Symbolism

Goal: To understand the function of imagery, symbolism, descriptive language, and personification in literary works

Common Core Standards, Grade 6

Reading—Literature: Key Ideas and Details

RL.6.2. Determine a theme or central idea of a text and how it is conveyed through particular details....

Common Core Standards, Grade 7

Reading—Literature: Key Ideas and Details

RL.7.2. Determine a theme or central idea of a text and analyze its development over the course of the text....

RL.7.3. Analyze how particular elements of a story or drama interact (e.g., how setting shapes the characters or plot).

Common Core Standards, Grade 8

Reading—Literature: Key Ideas and Details

RL.8.3. Analyze how particular lines of dialogue or incidents in a story or drama propel the action, reveal aspects of a character, or provoke a decision.

Student Activities Overview and Answer Key
Station 1

Students read a passage and identify the imagery used to describe characters, setting, and/or action.

Answers

Answers will vary depending upon the passage selected. Accept any reasonable responses.

Station 2

Students work individually and with their group to explain the meanings of several common symbols and how each symbol could be used in a story.

Answers

Answers will vary depending upon the symbols provided. Accept any reasonable responses.

Station 3

Students identify how a character would use each of his or her five senses in two different situations.

Answers

Answers will vary but need to be reasonable for each situation.

Station 4

Students write riddles describing well-known non-human characters that are examples of personification.

Answers

Answers will vary depending upon the character chosen. Accept any reasonable responses.

Materials List/Setup

Station 1	a short passage from a story that uses imagery to describe characters, setting, and/or action
Station 2	four or five pictures of common symbols (e.g., a bald eagle to represent the U.S. government)
Station 3	none
Station 4	none

Discussion Guide

To support students in reflecting on the activities and to gather some formative information about student learning, use the following prompts to facilitate a class discussion to "debrief" the station activities.

Prompts/Questions

1. List and describe three instances when authors use imagery to help readers understand a story.

2. Name a common symbol, identify its meaning, and explain why the symbol and the idea it represents are a good match.

3. Which of the five senses are easiest to include when using imagery in descriptive language? Explain your answer.

4. Why do you think authors use personification when writing about non-human characters?

Think, Pair, Share

Have students jot down their own responses to questions, then discuss with a partner (who was not in their station group), and then discuss as a whole class.

Suggested Appropriate Responses

1. Authors use imagery to establish character, setting, and/or action.

2. Answers will vary, depending upon the symbol chosen. Make sure that students make the connection between characteristics of the symbol and the idea it represents.

3. Answers will vary, but will most likely include sight and hearing as, unless he or she has a physical impairment, it is easy to describe what a character is able to see and hear. It may not always be as easy to describe what a character tastes, smells, or touches.

4. Personification enables authors to create non-human characters that readers are able to relate to more easily.

Possible Misunderstandings/Mistakes

- Forgetting to look for sensory descriptions beyond what the character sees and hears
- Forgetting that there are direct links between the characteristics of a symbol and the idea it represents
- Forgetting that while personification can make non-human things seem to be more like people, they actually do not have the characteristics being attributed to them

Reading—Literature
Set 4: Imagery and Symbolism

Station 1: Imagery

You will find a passage from a story at this station. Use the passage and this activity sheet to complete the station activity.

In literature, imagery refers to the use of descriptive language that creates pictures in the minds of readers. Writers use imagery to establish character, setting, and action in a story.

Read the story excerpt you find at this station. Use the table below to take notes.

Imagery		
Use the columns in this table to take notes about how the author uses imagery to help you "see" characters, visualize where the story is happening, or imagine the action that is taking place.		
Character	**Setting**	**Action**

After you've read the passage, share your notes with your group. How did the author use descriptive language? Did you find examples of use of imagery for all three columns? Did you find examples that other group members missed? Do you need to add anything to your notes?

Reading—Literature
Set 4: Imagery and Symbolism

Station 2: Symbolism

You will find several pictures of common symbols at this station. Follow the directions given on this activity sheet to explain what each symbol stands for and how it could be used in a story.

Symbolism means using an image to represent an idea. For example, when you see a picture of the character Smokey the Bear, you think of preventing forest fires. You would know without even reading it that a story featuring this famous symbol would have something to do with protecting forests.

Look at the pictures of common symbols at this station. Complete the chart below. Use the column on the left to name the symbol and the column on the right to explain what the symbol stands for.

Symbol	Meaning

Share your ideas about each symbol with your group. As a team, use the space below to brainstorm story ideas for each symbol.

_____

_____

_____

_____

_____

Reading—Literature
Set 4: Imagery and Symbolism

Station 3: Imagery and the Senses

At this station, you will identify how a character would use each of his or her five senses in two different situations.

Your five senses are sight, hearing, taste, touch, and smell. You use these senses to understand your surroundings and to make sense of events as they happen. Writers often include descriptions of what a character sees, hears, tastes, touches, or smells to keep the reader interested in the events in a story.

Read the situations described below. Decide how a character in a story would use his or her senses in each situation. Write a sentence describing how each sense would be used.

1. walking through a cemetery at midnight

    a. What would the character see? _____

    _____

    b. What would the character hear? _____

    _____

    c. What would the character taste? _____

    _____

    d. What would the character touch? _____

    _____

    e. What would the character smell? _____

    _____

continued

© 2011 Walch Education

Reading—Literature
Set 4: Imagery and Symbolism

2. seeing a movie at the theater

a. What would the character see? _____

_____

b. What would the character hear? _____

_____

c. What would the character taste? _____

_____

d. What would the character touch? _____

_____

e. What would the character smell? _____

_____

When you finish, share and discuss your responses with your group. As a team, choose one of these situations and write a four- to five-sentence paragraph that describes the event through the character's senses.

Reading—Literature
Set 4: Imagery and Symbolism

Station 4: Personification Riddle

Personification means giving human traits to non-human things. Writers use personification when the main characters of a story are animals or non-living things. The *Toy Story* movies are examples because the main characters behave like people do, but they are actually toys.

Think of a movie, book, or story you have read in which one or more characters behaved like a person, but were non-human. Choose one of these characters. Use the space below to brainstorm a list of things you know about the character, such as likes, dislikes, clothing worn, and/or physical description.

_____

_____

_____

_____

_____

Now use your ideas to write a three- to four-sentence riddle that describes the character. Be sure to include enough information so that someone reading the riddle could guess who the character is, but do not include the name of the character.

_____

_____

_____

_____

_____

When all group members have written a riddle, take turns reading them out loud. How many characters can you name? Does each riddle provide enough information for listeners to make correct guesses without giving the answer away too easily? How could you improve your riddle? Take a few minutes to edit your riddle before you turn it in.

Reading—Informational Text

Goal: To provide opportunities for students to develop concepts and skills related to finding information in a text using scanning and skimming techniques

Common Core Standards, Grade 6

Reading—Informational Text: Key Ideas and Details

RI.6.2.   Determine a central idea of a text and how it is conveyed through particular details....

Common Core Standards, Grade 7

Reading—Informational Text: Key Ideas and Details

RI.7.1.   Cite several pieces of textual evidence to support analysis of what the text says explicitly as well as inferences drawn from the text.

Reading—Informational Text: Craft and Structure

RI.7.6.   Determine an author's point of view or purpose in a text....

Common Core Standards, Grade 8

Reading—Informational Text: Key Ideas and Details

RI.8.1.   Cite the textual evidence that most strongly supports an analysis of what the text says explicitly as well as inferences drawn from the text.

RI.8.6.   Determine an author's point of view or purpose in a text and analyze how the author acknowledges and responds to conflicting evidence or viewpoints.

Student Activities Overview and Answer Key
Station 1

Students skim a short article to find the main idea and then scan the same article to find three specific pieces of information.

Answers

Main idea: Although most schools banned cell phones in the 1990s, people's attitudes about cell phones are changing and officials are being pressured to allow cell phones on campus.

1.   School officials believed they were being used by gang members and drug dealers.

2.   by texting test answers and photographing test papers

3.   as a safety measure

Station 2

Students scan the title and headings of a short article and write what they think the article is about. They compare their answers to those of other team members and then read the article to check their answers for accuracy.

Answers

This article describes ancient Greek inventions in the categories of tools and weapons, water technology, and mining. This information is contained in the title and the headings.

Station 3

Students practice their skills in finding information by identifying keywords in questions and scanning text to find the answers.

Answers

Keywords:	**Questions:**
1. marine animal, fish	1. backbone, fins
2. circulates through starfish's body	2. sea water
3. attached, starfish's arms	3. its feet

Station 4

Students practice their skills in finding information using a visual aid by examining a photograph and writing a caption.

Answers

Answers will vary. Accept any caption that reflects a reasonable interpretation of the photograph.

Materials List/Setup

Station 1	none
Station 2	none
Station 3	three different colored markers for each group member
Station 4	one copy of a photograph for each student (delete caption before copying)

Note: Photographs may come from a textbook, magazine, newspaper article or online collection such as the National Gallery of Art (www.nga.gov/collection/gallery/photo.shtm).

Discussion Guide

To support students in reflecting on the activities and to gather some formative information about student learning, use the following prompts to facilitate a class discussion to "debrief" the station activities.

Prompts/Questions

1. Describe what you are looking for when you skim text.
2. Describe what you are looking for when you scan text.
3. Discuss what you can learn from titles and headings.
4. Illustrate how keywords help you find information.

Think, Pair, Share

Have students jot down their own responses to questions, then discuss with a partner (who was not in their station group), and then discuss as a whole class.

Suggested Appropriate Responses

1. When readers skim, they are looking for the main idea of the text.
2. When readers scan, they are looking for specific information in the text.
3. Answer should include the fact that titles and headings give you a general idea of what the text is about, or the main idea.
4. Scanning for keywords helps readers find specific information quickly. Individual examples will vary.

Possible Misunderstandings/Mistakes

- Confusing the strategies skim and scan
- Assuming that readers skim or scan text instead of using both strategies
- Misidentifying keywords, e.g., choosing inconsequential words or leaving out important words

Reading—Informational Text
Set 1: Finding Information in a Text

Station 1: Skimming and Scanning

Use the article below to practice your skills in skimming and scanning text.

Skimming is used to quickly identify the main idea of a text. Skimming techniques include reading the title and the first sentence of each paragraph. Use these techniques to skim this article. Then write the main idea of the article in the space provided below.

The Cell Phone Issue

Many schools banned student use of cell phones on campus during the 1990s. This was because school officials believed that cell phones were mostly used by gang members or drug dealers. At the time, very few students owned cell phones, so no one questioned the rule.

People's attitudes about cell phones have changed since then. Thanks to lower costs and better technology, it seems as if everyone carries a cell phone today—even students in elementary school. Parents give cell phones to their children so they can contact them any time. Students use cell phones to stay in touch with friends. But cell phones may still be banned at school.

Some educators object to cell phones on campus because they believe that cell phones interrupt class. They don't want students taking calls or texting when they should be paying attention to a lesson. They also are afraid that students will cheat by texting test answers to one another or using the phone's camera to take and send pictures of test papers.

It's true that some students have abused the privilege of carrying a cell phone on campus. However, since the 9/11 attacks, more parents want schools to allow cell phones as a safety measure. In this case, schools often decide to allow cell phones, but say they must be turned off during class. What do you think? Should students be permitted to bring cell phones to school?

---

1. What is the main idea of this article? _____

_____

Scanning is used when you are looking for a specific piece of information in a text. Now scan the article to find the answers to the following questions.

2. Why were cell phones banned in schools in the 1990s? _____

_____

3. How do dishonest students cheat with cell phones? _____

_____

4. Why do some parents want school officials to allow cell phones? _____

_____

English Language Arts Station Activities for Common Core State Standards

Reading—Informational Text
Set 1: Finding Information in a Text

Station 2: Scanning Titles and Headings
Use the article below to practice your skills in finding information by scanning titles and headings.

This article is about innovation in Ancient Greece. <u>Don't read the article yet.</u> Scan it by reading the title and headings.

Inventions of Ancient Greece

The ancient Greeks were very clever. They made many discoveries starting in the 5th century and on through the Roman period. Many of these innovations were inspired by the need to improve weapons for warfare. Others were for peaceful purposes. What were some inventions of the ancient Greeks?

Tools and Weapons

Ancient Greeks invented many tools we still use today. For example, they created cranes, screws, odometers, and wheelbarrows. They are even said to have invented the shower! Weapons invented by ancient Greeks include the crossbow, catapults, and cannons.

Water Technology

Ancient Greeks needed to find ways to bring water to their cities. They did this by designing and building aqueducts. They also figured out ways to drain streets after heavy rains. They created sewer systems to remove wastewater. Ancient Greeks also invented fountains.

Mining

Athens became an important city-state. One reason it did was that there was a silver mine nearby. The ancient Greeks figured out how to mine underground ore. They washed it and then smelted it to produce silver. You can still see ancient washing tables at the site of the old silver mine.

---

1. Based upon your scan of this article, what do you think it is about? Explain your reasoning.

   _____

   _____

   _____

   _____

2. Compare your answer with your group members' answers. Are you all in agreement? Now read the article to see if your answer is correct.

Reading—Informational Text
Set 1: Finding Information in a Text

Station 3: Keywords

You will find colored markers at this station. Each member of your group needs three markers (choose three different colors). Use this activity sheet to practice your skills in finding information by identifying keywords in questions and scanning text to find the answers.

Questions about a text often include keywords. Keywords can help you find information when you skim the material. Read the three questions below. Highlight the keywords you find in each question. Assign a different color marker for each question by making a mark in that color on the line next to each question.

1. What does a marine animal need to have to be a fish? (color 1) _____

2. What circulates through a starfish's body? (color 2) _____

3. What is attached to a starfish's arms? (color 3) _____

Now read this paragraph about starfish. When you find a keyword for question 1, highlight it using color 1. When you find a keyword for question 2, highlight it using color 2. When you find a keyword for question 3, highlight it using color 3.

> You've seen pictures of starfish, but what do you really know about them? There are many strange facts about these marine animals. For example, starfish are not actually fish because they do not have backbones or fins. That's not all they're missing. Although starfish have mouths, they do not have heads. Starfish do not have brains and they do not have blood. Sea water circulates through their bodies instead. A last odd fact is that starfish may be the only animal whose feet are attached to their arms.

Write the answer to each question on the lines below.

1. What does a marine animal need to have to be a fish? _____

_____

2. What circulates through a starfish's body? _____

_____

3. What is attached to a starfish's arms? _____

_____

Reading—Informational Text
Set 1: Finding Information in a Text

Station 4: Finding Information Using Visual Aids

You will find copies of a photograph at this station. Each member of your group needs to take one copy of the photograph. Use this activity sheet and the photograph to practice your skills in finding information using a visual aid.

Photographs, charts, graphs, and maps provide information about text. But readers often forget to take time to examine graphic aids carefully. Look at the photograph you found at this station. Answer the following questions.

1. What or who is the main subject of this photograph?

   _____

   _____

2. What is happening in this photograph?

   _____

   _____

3. When do you think this photograph was taken?

   _____

   _____

4. Where do you think this photograph was taken?

   _____

   _____

5. Why do you think this photograph was taken?

   _____

   _____

6. A caption is text that describes a visual aid. Write a caption for the photograph.

   _____

   _____

   Share and discuss your caption with members of your group.

English Language Arts Station Activities for Common Core State Standards

Reading—Informational Text

Set 2: Reading Strategies

Goal: To understand and apply various strategies used while reading, including visualizing, making connections, re-reading, questioning, and summarizing

Common Core Standards, Grade 6

Reading—Informational Text: Key Ideas and Details

RI.6.1. Cite textual evidence to support analysis of what the text says explicitly as well as inferences drawn from the text.

Reading—Informational Text: Range of Reading and Level of Text Complexity

RI.6.10. By the end of the year, read and comprehend literary nonfiction in the grades 6–8 text complexity band proficiently, with scaffolding as needed at the high end of the range.

Common Core Standards, Grade 7

Reading—Informational Text: Key Ideas and Details

RI.7.1. Cite several pieces of textual evidence to support analysis of what the text says explicitly as well as inferences drawn from the text.

Reading—Informational Text: Range of Reading and Level of Text Complexity

RI.7.10. By the end of the year, read and comprehend literary nonfiction in the grades 6–8 text complexity band proficiently, with scaffolding as needed at the high end of the range.

Student Activities Overview and Answer Key

Station 1

Students work with their groups to complete a K-W-L chart as they read a short article.

Answers

Answers will vary depending upon the assigned article. Accept any reasonable responses.

Station 2

Students complete an SQ3R chart as they read a short article.

Answers

Answers will vary depending upon the assigned article. Accept any reasonable responses.

Station 3

Students complete a Double-Entry Notes chart as they read a short article.

Answers

Answers will vary depending upon the assigned article. Accept any reasonable responses.

Station 4

Students write a short letter to the teacher reflecting on the pre-reading and reading strategies they are learning.

Answers

Answers will vary. Accept any responses that include helpful strategies, less helpful strategies, and the most important thing the student has learned about reading.

Materials List/Setup

Note: You need a different short article for each station.

Station 1   short (one page or less) newspaper or magazine article

Station 2   short (one page or less) newspaper or magazine article

Station 3   short (one page or less) newspaper or magazine article

Station 4   none

Discussion Guide

To support students in reflecting on the activities and to gather some formative information about student learning, use the following prompts to facilitate a class discussion to "debrief" the station activities.

Prompts/Questions

1. Choose the reading strategy charts you liked best. Explain.
2. Choose the reading strategy charts you liked least. Explain.
3. Describe how you will use these strategies in other classes.
4. Discuss the most important reading strategy you've learned in this class.

Think, Pair, Share

Have students jot down their own responses to questions, then discuss with a partner (who was not in their station group), and then discuss as a whole class.

Suggested Appropriate Responses

1–4. Answers will vary.

Possible Misunderstandings/Mistakes

- Assuming use of these strategies is limited to an English/Language Arts class
- Not understanding that they can use different strategies for different kinds of reading
- Forgetting to continue to use these strategies

Reading—Informational Text
Set 2: Reading Strategies

Station 1: K-W-L Charts

You will find a short article at this station. You will use the K-W-L chart on the next page to work with your group to complete the three columns.

A K-W-L chart guides you in reading and understanding a text. Discuss the following questions with your group and fill out the three columns of your chart.

Know

What do you already know about the topic of the text you will read? Brainstorm a list of keywords and ideas. Write them in the first column. Discuss your list with the group. Organize your list into general categories.

Want

What do you want to know about this topic? Preview the text, looking at the title, headings, visual aids, and other items that provide clues about the content of the text. Discuss what you want to learn with your group. Write a list of things you want to learn, phrasing each item as a question. Put your questions in order of importance, most important first. Then read the article.

Learn

What did you learn from your reading? Make a list of things you learned. Compare it to your list of questions in the "W" column. Did you find all the information you wanted to learn? Discuss with your group.

continued

Reading—Informational Text
Set 2: Reading Strategies

K-W-L Chart

Title of text: _____

What We <u>Know</u>	What We <u>Want</u> to Know	What We <u>Learned</u>

Reading—Informational Text
Set 2: Reading Strategies

Station 2: SQ3R

You will find a short article at this station. You will use the SQ3R chart on the next page as you read the article.

The SQ3R reading strategy takes a little more time to complete, but researchers say that students who use this strategy remember much more about what they read than students who do not use SQ3R. This activity helps you practice these skills.

- **Survey:** Preview the text. Make a list of keywords you find.

- **Question:** What questions are raised by the survey? List these questions in the second column.

- **Read:** Look for answers to the questions you wrote in the second column. List the answers in the third column.

- **Recall:** Think about what you've just read. List the most important information in the fourth column.

- **Reflect:** Think about ways what you have read are connected to what you already know or to your previous experience. Write 2–3 summarizing statements in the fifth column.

continued

Reading—Informational Text
Set 2: Reading Strategies

SQ3R

Title of text: _____

S Survey	Q Question	R Read	R Recall	R Reflect

Reading—Informational Text
Set 2: Reading Strategies

Station 3: Double-Entry Notes

You will find a short article at this station. You will use the Double-Entry Notes chart on the next page as you read the article.

Taking useful notes is a tough skill to learn. Students often take pages of notes that they never use again because the notes make no sense later. Double-Entry Notes charts help you remember to write down just the most important ideas and provide a place for you to explain why each note is important. This style of note-taking is very helpful when you need to review for a project or test.

Read the short article at this station. As you read, write the main ideas in the column on the left. Each time you write something here, take time to write a short explanation about why you think this idea is important in the column on the right.

When you finish, share and discuss your responses with your group.

continued

Reading—Informational Text
Set 2: Reading Strategies

Double-Entry Notes

Title of text: _____

What I Read	What I Think

Reading—Informational Text
Set 2: Reading Strategies

Station 4: A Letter to Your Teacher

Use this activity sheet to write a short letter to your teacher. In this letter, reflect on the pre-reading and reading strategies you are learning.

When business owners are asked to list the top five skills they look for in new employees, they nearly always include good reading comprehension. They need to know that their employees will be able to read and understand all the articles, memos, e-mails, and other written communication sent to them.

Use the space below to write a letter to your teacher. In this letter, list the strategies that are most helpful to you and explain why. Then list the strategies that are not helpful or that are confusing and explain why. Finish up by telling your teacher the most important thing you've learned about reading in this class.

Reading—Informational Text

Set 3: Reading for Meaning

Goal: To provide opportunities for students to practice various strategies for increasing reading comprehension, including interpreting idioms, differentiating between fact and opinion, drawing conclusions, and using context clues

Common Core Standards, Grade 6

Reading—Informational Text: Key Ideas and Details

RI.6.1. Cite textual evidence to support analysis of what the text says explicitly as well as inferences drawn from the text.

RI.6.2. Determine a central idea of a text and how it is conveyed through particular details....

Reading—Informational Text: Craft and Structure

RI.6.4. Determine the meaning of words and phrases as they are used in a text, including figurative, connotative, and technical meanings.

RI.6.6. Determine an author's point of view or purpose in a text and explain how it is conveyed in the text.

Reading—Informational Text: Integration of Knowledge and Ideas

RI.6.8. Trace and evaluate the argument and specific claims in a text, distinguishing claims that are supported by reasons and evidence from claims that are not.

Language: Vocabulary Acquisition and Use

L.6.4. Determine or clarify the meaning of unknown and multiple-meaning words and phrases based on grade 6 reading and content, choosing flexibly from a range of strategies.

　　a. Use context (e.g., the overall meaning of a sentence or paragraph; a word's position or function in a sentence) as a clue to the meaning of a word or phrase.

　　b. Use common, grade-appropriate Greek or Latin affixes and roots as clues to the meaning of a word (e.g., *audience, auditory, audible*).

L.6.5. Demonstrate understanding of figurative language, word relationships, and nuances in word meanings.

Common Core Standards, Grade 7

Reading—Informational Text: Key Ideas and Details

RI.7.1. Cite several pieces of textual evidence to support analysis of what the text says explicitly as well as inferences drawn from the text.

RI.7.2. Determine two or more central ideas in a text....

Reading—Informational Text: Craft and Structure

RI.7.4. Determine the meaning of words and phrases as they are used in a text, including figurative, connotative, and technical meanings; analyze the impact of a specific word choice on meaning and tone.

RI.7.6. Determine an author's point of view or purpose in a text and analyze how the author distinguishes his or her position from that of others.

Reading—Informational Text: Integration of Knowledge and Ideas

RI.7.8. Trace and evaluate the argument and specific claims in a text, assessing whether the reasoning is sound and the evidence is relevant and sufficient to support the claims.

Language: Vocabulary Acquisition and Use

L.7.4. Determine or clarify the meaning of unknown and multiple-meaning words and phrases based on *grade 7 reading and content*, choosing flexibly from a range of strategies.

    a. Use context (e.g., the overall meaning of a sentence or paragraph; a word's position or function in a sentence) as a clue to the meaning of a word or phrase.

    b. Use common, grade-appropriate Greek or Latin affixes and roots as clues to the meaning of a word (e.g., *belligerent, bellicose, rebel*).

L.7.5. Demonstrate understanding of figurative language, word relationships, and nuances in word meanings.

    a. Interpret figures of speech (e.g., literary, biblical, and mythological allusions) in context.

Common Core Standards, Grade 8

Reading—Informational Text: Key Ideas and Details

RI.8.1. Cite the textual evidence that most strongly supports an analysis of what the text says explicitly as well as inferences drawn from the text.

RI.8.2. Determine a central idea of a text and analyze its development over the course of the text, including its relationship to supporting ideas....

Reading—Informational Text: Craft and Structure

RI.8.4. Determine the meaning of words and phrases as they are used in a text, including figurative, connotative, and technical meanings; analyze the impact of specific word choices on meaning and tone, including analogies or allusions to other texts.

RI.8.6. Determine an author's point of view or purpose in a text and analyze how the author acknowledges and responds to conflicting evidence or viewpoints.

Reading—Informational Text: Integration of Knowledge and Ideas

RI.8.8. Delineate and evaluate the argument and specific claims in a text, assessing whether the reasoning is sound and the evidence is relevant and sufficient; recognize when irrelevant evidence is introduced.

Language: Vocabulary Acquisition and Use

L.8.4. Determine or clarify the meaning of unknown and multiple-meaning words or phrases based on *grade 8 reading and content*, choosing flexibly from a range of strategies.

    a. Use context (e.g., the overall meaning of a sentence or paragraph; a word's position or function in a sentence) as a clue to the meaning of a word or phrase.

    b. Use common, grade-appropriate Greek or Latin affixes and roots as clues to the meaning of a word (e.g., *precede, recede, secede*).

L.8.5. Demonstrate understanding of figurative language, word relationships, and nuances in word meanings.

    a. Interpret figures of speech (e.g. verbal irony, puns) in context.

    b. Use the relationship between particular words to better understand each of the words.

Student Activities Overview and Answer Key
Station 1

Students illustrate the literal meaning of an idiom, explain its figurative meaning, and use the idiom in a sentence.

Answers

Answers will vary depending upon the idiom selected. Accept any reasonable responses.

Station 2

Students work with their group to identify facts and opinions found in a printed advertisement.

Answers

Answers will vary depending upon the advertisement used. Accept any reasonable responses.

Station 3

Students complete a Drawing Conclusions chart as they read a newspaper editorial.

Answers

Answers will vary depending upon the assigned editorial. Accept any reasonable responses.

Station 4

Students identify context clues they can use to determine the meanings of unfamiliar words.

Answers

Students will color-code unfamiliar words according to how they are used. Words used as examples will be red; synonyms will be blue; antonyms will be yellow; and explanation words will be green. Here, words that students should color red (examples) are UNDERLINED ONCE. Blue words are UNDERLINED TWICE. Yellow words are CIRCLED; and green words are in RECTANGLES.

1. Lucinda is a bookish student, very well-read.

2. The new football team exceeded everyone's hopes—no one underachieved in this group!

3. Her behavior was outrageous, including screaming at her friends and crying for no reason.

4. When my father was transferred, it meant he needed to work at a different store.

5. After taking biology, his interest in science did not diminish; instead, it grew.

6. When the generals declared the truce, fighting stopped immediately.

7. Our teacher is nearly always amiable; for example, she is friendly and cares about her students.

8. David was persuaded to taste the sandwich after he was convinced that it was fresh.

Materials List/Setup

Station 1   6 to 8 index cards, with a different idiom printed on each card
(If possible, use idioms that appear in assigned readings.)

Station 2   copies of a printed advertisement

Station 3   copies of a newspaper editorial
(*Note:* The online version of a local or regional newspaper is a good resource for editorials your students will be able to relate to.)

Station 4   colored markers (red, blue, yellow, green—one set per group member)

Discussion Guide

To support students in reflecting on the activities and to gather some formative information about student learning, use the following prompts to facilitate a class discussion to "debrief" the station activities.

Prompts/Questions

1. Describe why readers are sometimes confused by idioms.

2. Why is it important to understand the difference between a fact and an opinion?

3. What are you asked to do when you read between the lines?

4. Identify four types of context clues.

Think, Pair, Share

Have students jot down their own responses to questions, then discuss with a partner (who was not in their station group), and then discuss as a whole class.

Suggested Appropriate Responses

1. because idioms do not mean what they literally say

2. Facts can be verified; opinions cannot. This leads to confusion when a reader does not understand the difference.

3. draw a conclusion

4. example, synonym, antonym, explanation

Possible Misunderstandings/Mistakes

- Interpreting an idiom literally
- Forgetting to verify that a factual statement is actually true
- Forgetting to look for context clues when an unfamiliar word is encountered in reading

Reading—Informational Text
Set 3: Reading for Meaning

Station 1: Idioms

You will find 6 to 8 index cards at this station. You will use the idiom printed on one card and this activity sheet to complete the station activity.

An idiom is a figurative expression. It does not mean what it literally says. For example, when a person says, "I don't want to talk much today because I have a frog in my throat," the figurative meaning is that she doesn't want to talk because her voice sounds croaky, not because she's literally tried to swallow a frog!

Turn the index cards face down. Each group member chooses one card and reads the idiom printed on the card. Use the space provided here to draw a picture of the literal meaning of the idiom.

Explain what the idiom means

Use the lines below to explain the idiom's figurative meaning.

_____

_____

Use the idiom in a sentence

Use the lines below here to use the idiom in a sentence.

_____

_____

Reading—Informational Text
Set 3: Reading for Meaning

Station 2: Fact vs. Opinion

You will find a printed advertisement at this station. You will use the chart below to list the facts and opinions you find in the advertisement.

To really understand a text, you must be able to tell the difference between facts and opinions. A statement is a fact when you can answer yes to these questions:

- Is this statement true?
- Can I prove that this statement is true?

When you cannot answer yes to both questions, the statement is an opinion.

Read the advertisement. Think about each statement and ask yourself the two questions. If your answers are yes, write the statement in the column marked "Fact." If your answer to one or both questions is no, write the statement in the column marked "Opinion."

Discuss your findings with your group. Are there different ideas about what is a fact and what is an opinion? Try to reach agreement about each statement.

Fact	Opinion

Reading—Informational Text
Set 3: Reading for Meaning

Station 3: Drawing Conclusions

You will find a newspaper editorial at this station. Use the Drawing Conclusions chart below as you read the editorial.

When you read, simply getting the facts or finding what someone else thinks isn't enough. You also need to read between the lines to figure out what the author is really saying. You do this by identifying important statements in the reading, thinking about what you know about these statements, and then deciding what the statements mean. This is called drawing a conclusion.

Read the editorial at this station. As you read, write the main ideas in the column labeled "Statements I Read." After you finish reading, look at the statements you wrote. Use the middle column to write what you know about these statements. Finally, write your conclusion in the column on the right. Consider the following questions as you write your conclusion: What is this editorial about? What does the writer want you to think? What do you really think? When you finish, share and discuss your responses with your group.

Drawing Conclusions

Statements I Read	What I Know	My Conclusion

Reading—Informational Text
Set 3: Reading for Meaning

Station 4: Context Clues

You will find colored markers at this station. Each member of your group needs four markers (red, blue, yellow, green). Use this activity sheet to identify context clues that can help you figure out the meanings of unfamiliar words.

You will often come across unfamiliar words as you read. Authors know this, and often include hints about the meanings of these words. The hints are called **context clues**. Four common context clues are the following:

- **Examples (red):** Look for words or phrases like "such as," "including," and "for example."
- **Synonyms (blue):** Look in the sentence for a word with the same meaning.
- **Antonyms (yellow):** Look in the sentence for a word with the opposite meaning.
- **Explanations (green):** Look for a phrase that explains the meaning of the word.

Read the sentences below. When you see an unfamiliar word and a context clue, highlight both using the color indicated in the list above.

1. Lucinda is a bookish student, very well-read.

2. The new football team exceeded everyone's hopes—no one underachieved in this group!

3. Her behavior was outrageous, including screaming at her friends and crying for no reason.

4. When my father was transferred, it meant he needed to work at a different store.

5. After taking biology, his interest in science did not diminish; instead, it grew.

6. When the generals declared the truce, fighting stopped immediately.

7. Our teacher is nearly always amiable; for example, she is friendly and cares about her students.

8. David was persuaded to taste the sandwich after he was convinced that it was fresh.

Reading—Informational Text

Goal: To explore connections between two or more texts and to identify personal connections to various literary and artistic works

Common Core Standards, Grade 6

Reading—Literature: Key Ideas and Details

RL.6.2.   Determine a theme or central idea of a text and how it is conveyed through particular details; provide a summary of the text distinct from personal opinions or judgments.

Reading—Informational Text: Integration of Knowledge and Ideas

RI.6.9.   Compare and contrast one author's presentation of events with that of another (e.g., a memoir written by and a biography on the same person).

Reading—Informational Text: Key Ideas and Details

RI.6.1.   Cite textual evidence to support analysis of what the text says explicitly as well as inferences drawn from the text.

RI.6.2.   Determine a central idea of a text and how it is conveyed through particular details; provide a summary of the text distinct from personal opinions or judgments.

Common Core Standards, Grade 7

Reading—Literature: Key Ideas and Details

RL.7.2.   Determine a theme or central idea of a text and analyze its development over the course of the text; provide an objective summary of the text.

Reading—Informational Text: Key Ideas and Details

RI.7.1.   Cite several pieces of textual evidence to support analysis of what the text says explicitly as well as inferences drawn from the text.

Reading—Informational Text: Integration of Knowledge and Ideas

RI.7.9.   Analyze how two or more authors writing about the same topic shape their presentations of key information by emphasizing different evidence or advancing different interpretations of facts.

Common Core Standards, Grade 8

Reading—Literature: Key Ideas and Details

RL.8.2.   Determine a theme or central idea of a text ... [and] provide an objective summary of the text.

Reading—Informational Text: Integration of Knowledge and Ideas

RI.8.9. Analyze a case in which two or more texts provide conflicting information on the same topic and identify where the texts disagree on matters of fact or interpretation.

Reading—Informational Text: Key Ideas and Details

RI.8.1. Cite the textual evidence that most strongly supports an analysis of what the text says explicitly as well as inferences drawn from the text.

Student Activities Overview and Answer Key

Station 1

Students compare and contrast two news stories (from different sources) written about the same topic.

Answers

Answers will vary depending upon the readings selected. Accept any reasonable responses.

Station 2

Students read a local news story and write an explanation about how the topic of the story affects them personally.

Answers

Answers will vary depending upon the local news story selected. Accept any reasonable responses.

Station 3

Students skim the headlines and images on the front page of a newspaper and choose one story to read carefully. Before reading, students write a sentence explaining what they think the story is about. After reading, students write a brief explanation of what the story was actually about.

Answers

Answers will vary depending upon the story selected. Accept any reasonable responses.

Station 4

Students identify the themes for a favorite book, movie, song, and television show, and explain why these themes appeal to them.

Answers

Answers will vary depending upon the items selected by each student. Accept any reasonable responses.

Materials List/Setup

Station 1	copies of two newspaper stories (from different sources) written about the same topic
Station 2	copies of a newspaper story about a local event or topic
Station 3	copies of the front section of a newspaper
Station 4	none

Discussion Guide

To support students in reflecting on the activities and to gather some formative information about student learning, use the following prompts to facilitate a class discussion to "debrief" the station activities.

Prompts/Questions

1. What can you learn by comparing and contrasting two writing samples about the same topic?

2. Why is it often easier to relate to a story about a local issue than it is to relate to a story about a national or international issue?

3. How do titles and graphics influence your choices about what to read?

4. What can you learn about yourself by exploring the themes of your favorite literary or artistic works?

Think, Pair, Share

Have students jot down their own responses to questions, then discuss with a partner (who was not in their station group), and then discuss as a whole class.

Suggested Appropriate Responses

1. Most issues have more than one point of view. By reading more than one article about the same topic, readers gather more information and can make better decisions about the issue.

2. Local issues often impact students' friends, family, and neighbors. It's easier to make a personal connection when you know the people involved.

3. Catchy titles or images attract the reader's attention and appear to be more interesting than stories with a boring title or no images. But this can be deceiving.

4. Identifying patterns in themes that appeal to an individual can tell about that person's current emotional state or belief system. For example, a person who prefers themes about illness, death, or violence may be depressed or without hope, while a person who prefers themes about friendship, love, or the triumph of good over evil may have a sunnier outlook on life in general.

Possible Misunderstandings/Mistakes

- Thinking readers need just one information source before making up their minds about an issue
- Making false predictions about the content or value of a piece of writing based upon catchy titles or graphics
- Thinking that a literary or artistic work can have just one theme

English Language Arts Station Activities for Common Core State Standards

Reading—Informational Text
Set 4: Connections Between Texts

Station 1: Compare and Contrast

You will find copies of two newspaper stories at this station. You will use the stories and this activity sheet to complete the station activity.

One good way to analyze two or more writing samples about the same topic is to compare and contrast them. Finding the similarities and differences will give you a lot of information about each item you read.

Read the newspaper stories you find at this station. Although they are both about the same topic, these stories come from different sources. Use the chart on the next page to answer the questions. Then write a short description to summarize the similarities and differences between the two.

Once you have completed the chart on the next page, share and discuss your answers with your group. Compare and contrast your summaries during the discussion. Use the space below to take notes about the discussion.

Reading—Informational Text
Set 4: Connections Between Texts

Compare and Contrast

Question	Story 1	Story 2
What is the author's purpose?		
What tone does the author use?		
What is the theme?		
What supporting evidence or facts are provided?		
What opinion is expressed?		
What style of writing is used?		
Summary of similarities and differences:		

Reading—Informational Text
Set 4: Connections Between Texts

Station 2: Generating a Reader's Response

You will find copies of a local news story at this station. Use the news story and this activity sheet to complete the station activity.

National and international news are important to read. But it may seem that this kind of news doesn't have much to do with your everyday life. Local news, on the other hand, often has a direct impact on everyone in the community. For example, if the city's public pool is being closed because of budget cuts, many of your friends and neighbors, and you personally, might be affected in several ways. Teenagers and adults will lose their jobs. People will need to find a new place where they can go to cool off or exercise.

Read the local news story and write a personal response about how this event affects you, your family, and your friends. Use the chart on the next page.

Then discuss your chart with your group. Compare answers for similarities and differences. Overall, is this event positive for your community or negative? Explain.

continued

Reading—Informational Text
Set 4: Connections Between Texts

Story title: _____

Summarize the event in one sentence: _____

_____

Use the columns below to explain how this event affects you, your family, and your friends.

Impact on Me	Impact on My Family	Impact on My Friends

Reading—Informational Text
Set 4: Connections Between Texts

Station 3: Making Predictions about Text

You will find copies of the front section of a newspaper at this station. Use the newspaper section to complete this station activity.

You read a book starting with page one, but how do you decide where to begin reading a newspaper? Most readers usually look at the front page of the newspaper first, but even then, there are several stories to choose from. Newspaper editors often put the most important stories at the top of the page, but for many readers, it's a catchy title or interesting image that will capture their attention and get them to read that story first.

1. Look at the newspaper section. Begin by skimming all headlines and images on the front page. Choose one story to read carefully. Before you start to read, use the lines below to write a sentence explaining what you think the story is going to be about and why it interests you.

   _____

   _____

2. Now read the story. When you finish reading, write a short summary of the story below.

   _____

   _____

   _____

   _____

   _____

3. How accurate was your prediction? Were you able to figure out what the story was actually about before you read it? Why or why not?

   _____

   _____

   _____

   _____

   _____

Discuss this activity with your group. How many of you decided to read the same story? Why was this story interesting to your group members? How many of you decided to read different stories? Why? How accurate were the groups' predictions?

Reading—Informational Text
Set 4: Connections Between Texts

Station 4: Themes in Literary and Artistic Works

The **theme** of a book, play, movie, television show, or other work of art is a central idea or broad message that is repeated or supported throughout the literary work or performance. It's even possible to have more than one theme. For example, in Louis Sachar's book *Holes*, there are three themes: the impact of fate and history on people's lives; the importance of friendship; and having compassion for others, even people you don't like. The play *Romeo and Juliet* also has several themes related to love, violence, and death.

Think of your favorite books, movies, songs, and television shows. List the title of each in the chart below. Write at least one theme for each item you listed.

Title	Theme
Book:	
Movie:	
Song:	
Television show:	

continued

Reading—Informational Text
Set 4: Connections Between Texts

Look at the themes you have written in the chart. Are any of the themes repeated in more than one title, or are they all different? Think about what makes each of these items a favorite for you. Explain why you chose these favorites.

_____

_____

_____

_____

_____

When you are finished, exchange papers with another group member and read his or her answers. What are the themes for this person's favorites? Are the answers what you expected, or do some answers surprise you? What can you learn about the person by reading these answers?

Writing

Set 1: Prewriting

Goal: To discuss the importance of writing and identify the writing process

Common Core Standards, Grade 6

Writing: Production and Distribution of Writing

W.6.4. Produce clear and coherent writing in which the development, organization, and style are appropriate to task, purpose, and audience.

Common Core Standards, Grade 7

Writing: Production and Distribution of Writing

W.7.4. Produce clear and coherent writing in which the development, organization, and style are appropriate to task, purpose, and audience.

Common Core Standards, Grade 8

Writing: Production and Distribution of Writing

W.8.4. Produce clear and coherent writing in which the development, organization, and style are appropriate to task, purpose, and audience.

Student Activities Overview and Answer Key
Station 1

Students brainstorm a list of at least 30 ideas related to a topic.

Answers

Answers will vary depending upon the topic. Accept any reasonable responses.

Station 2

Students use a mind map to organize ideas around a main topic.

Answers

Answers will vary depending upon the topic. Accept any reasonable responses.

Station 3

Students use freewriting to generate ideas about a main topic.

Answers

Answers will vary upon the topic. Accept any reasonable responses.

Station 4

Students answer questions designed to identify the intended audience and purpose for an assigned topic.

Answers

Answers will vary depending upon the writing samples provided. Accept any reasonable responses.

Materials List/Setup

Station 1   teacher-assigned topic for brainstorming, two sheets of notebook paper for each student

Station 2   teacher-assigned topic for clustering, one sheet of drawing paper for each student

Station 3   teacher-assigned topic for freewriting, one sheet of notebook paper, and one highlighter for each student

Station 4   teacher-assigned writing topic

Discussion Guide

To support students in reflecting on the activities and to gather some formative information about student learning, use the following prompts to facilitate a class discussion to "debrief" the station activities.

Prompts/Questions

1. Discuss why the length of a brainstorming list can be important when you prewrite.

2. Compare and contrast using a mind map with making a brainstorming list.

3. Explain why you need to highlight ideas after you freewrite.

4. Analyze how knowing your audience and purpose affects what you write.

Think, Pair, Share

Have students jot down their own responses to questions, then discuss with a partner (who was not in their station group), and then discuss as a whole class.

Suggested Appropriate Responses

1. Short brainstorming lists tend to include just the obvious ideas. Longer lists encourage more creative thinking.

2. Mind mapping encourages you to start thinking right away in terms of subtopics and supporting information. In brainstorming, subtopics and supporting information are not organized in any particular way until after the list is completed.

3. When you freewrite, you are supposed to put down anything that comes to mind without doing any editing. Highlighting helps you begin to see ways you can organize your ideas.

4. When you think your only reading audience is a teacher and your purpose for writing is a grade, you will write just to please the teacher. However, when you write for other readers, you also need to take their skills and interests into account before you write.

Possible Misunderstandings/Mistakes

- Thinking there is just one effective strategy for prewriting
- Self-editing while freewriting
- Thinking that the teacher is their sole writing audience

Writing
Set 1: Prewriting

Station 1: Brainstorming

Your teacher will assign a topic to use to complete this station's brainstorming activity. Use the topic, two sheets of writing paper, and this activity sheet to complete the station activity.

The writing process consists of several steps. Before you actually begin to write a story or essay, you need to spend some time planning what you will write about. This is called **prewriting**. One prewriting strategy is called **brainstorming**, which means creating a list of ideas about a topic.

1. On a separate sheet of paper, write a list of at least 30 ideas related to the assigned topic. Spend at least 10 minutes creating your list. Write down every idea you have, no matter how small or silly it seems.

2. Use another sheet of paper to organize your brainstorming ideas into categories that make sense to you.

3. Give each category a title. List each title below and write a sentence about it.

_____

_____

_____

_____

_____

_____

_____

_____

_____

After you've written your sentences, discuss the process with your group. What strategies did you use to come up with 30 ideas? Compare and contrast the categories you created with the categories created by other members of your group.

Writing
Set 1: Prewriting

Station 2: Organizing Ideas

Your teacher will assign a topic to use to complete this station's activity on organizing ideas. Use the topic, one sheet of drawing paper, and this activity sheet to complete the station activity.

The writing process consists of several steps. Before you actually begin to write a story or essay, you need to spend time planning what you will write about. This is called **prewriting**. Organizing your ideas is an important prewriting task. Mind maps or idea maps are one way to get organized.

1. Take one sheet of drawing paper. Write the assigned topic in the center of the paper and draw a circle around it.

2. Think of ideas related to this topic. These are called subtopics. Write each subtopic on the drawing paper. Circle each one and draw a line to link each subtopic to the main topic.

3. Think of ideas related to each subtopic. Write these ideas on the drawing paper, circle each one, and connect them to their subtopics.

4. Your mind map should look like a web. Which of the subtopics are most interesting to you? Write your answer below along with a sentence explaining why you chose these subtopics.

_____

_____

_____

_____

_____

Exchange your mind map with another group member. Read that person's map. Does it make sense to you? Do you have any questions or suggestions? Do you see ideas you'd like to add to your mind map? Discuss your thoughts with this group member.

Writing
Set 1: Prewriting

Station 3: Freewriting

Your teacher will assign a topic to use to complete this station's activity on freewriting. Use the topic, one sheet of notebook paper, and this activity sheet to complete the station activity.

Prewriting is an important first step in the writing process because it helps you think about what you want to write about. One prewriting strategy is called **freewriting**. This strategy is helpful because you need to think of a lot of ideas about your topic in a short period of time.

When you freewrite, you write for 10 minutes without stopping. Even if you run out of ideas, you need to keep writing—new ideas will come to you. Focus on ideas and do not worry about grammar or spelling.

1. Take one sheet of notebook paper. Write the assigned topic at the top of the paper.

2. Freewrite about the assigned topic for 10 minutes.

3. When 10 minutes have passed, read over what you have written. Use a highlighter to mark the most interesting or important ideas.

Share your highlighted ideas with your group. Listen carefully as your group members share what they highlighted. Many ideas may be the same, but there will also be ideas just one person highlighted. Discuss these different ideas as a group. How could they be used to write an interesting story or essay?

Writing
Set 1: Prewriting

Station 4: Audience and Purpose

Use the topic assigned by your teacher to complete this station activity.

Identifying your reading audience and the purpose for the writing is an important prewriting task. Knowing this information can change what you write or how you write it. For example, when writing thank-you notes for birthday gifts, the note you write to your grandparents will probably be very different from the note you send to your best friend.

Answer the questions below and on the next page to identify the audience and purpose for the writing topic assigned by your teacher. When you are finished, exchange papers with another group member and read his or her answers. Although you are writing about the same topic, you may have answered several questions differently. Discuss these differences to understand how a writer's point of view affects his or her work.

Audience Questions	My Answers
1. Who will be reading this piece of writing? (List all possible readers.)	
2. What information do I want to share with my reader(s)?	
3. How will my audience use this information?	
4. What do my readers already think about the topic I am writing about?	

continued

Writing
Set 1: Prewriting

Purpose Questions	My Answers
1. How much information do I need to share?	
2. What are the most important ideas to include?	
3. How will I organize my information?	
4. What tone or writing style do I need to use?	

Writing

Goal: To explore the different types of writing, including narrative, descriptive, informative, and opinion

Common Core Standards, Grade 6

Writing: Text Types and Purposes

W.6.3. Write narratives to develop real or imagined experiences or events using effective technique, relevant descriptive details, and well-structured event sequences.

   d. Use precise words and phrases, relevant descriptive details, and sensory language to convey experiences and events.

Writing: Production and Distribution of Writing

W.6.4. Produce clear and coherent writing in which the development, organization, and style are appropriate to task, purpose, and audience.

W.6.5. With some guidance and support from peers and adults, develop and strengthen writing as needed by planning, revising, editing, rewriting, or trying a new approach.

Common Core Standards, Grade 7

Writing: Text Types and Purposes

W.7.3. Write narratives to develop real or imagined experiences or events using effective technique, relevant descriptive details, and well-structured event sequences.

   d. Use precise words and phrases, relevant descriptive details, and sensory language to capture the action and convey experiences and events.

Writing: Production and Distribution of Writing

W.7.4. Produce clear and coherent writing in which the development, organization, and style are appropriate to task, purpose, and audience.

W.7.5. With some guidance and support from peers and adults, develop and strengthen writing as needed by planning, revising, editing, rewriting, or trying a new approach, focusing on how well purpose and audience have been addressed.

Common Core Standards, Grade 8

Writing: Text Types and Purposes

W.8.3. Write narratives to develop real or imagined experiences or events using effective technique, relevant descriptive details, and well-structured event sequences.

   d. Use precise words and phrases, relevant descriptive details, and sensory language to capture the action and convey experiences and events.

Writing: Production and Distribution of Writing

W.8.4. Produce clear and coherent writing in which the development, organization, and style are appropriate to task, purpose, and audience.

W.8.5. With some guidance and support from peers and adults, develop and strengthen writing as needed by planning, revising, editing, rewriting, or trying a new approach, focusing on how well purpose and audience have been addressed.

Common Core Standards, Grade 6

Reading—Informational Text: Craft and Structure

RI.6.6. Determine an author's point of view or purpose in a text and explain how it is conveyed in the text.

Common Core Standards, Grade 7

Reading—Informational Text: Craft and Structure

RI.7.6. Determine an author's point of view or purpose in a text and analyze how the author distinguishes his or her position from that of others.

Common Core Standards, Grade 8

Reading—Informational Text: Craft and Structure

RI.8.6. Determine an author's point of view or purpose in a text and analyze how the author acknowledges and responds to conflicting evidence or viewpoints.

Student Activities Overview and Answer Key
Station 1

Students write a complete narrative story in 10 sentences or less.

Answers

Answers will vary depending upon the topic. Reasonable responses will include basic elements of plot and tell a complete, brief story.

Station 2

Students write a detailed description of a mystery object.

Answers

Answers will vary. Acceptable responses include sensory language and vivid details.

Station 3

Students identify a piece of informative writing and explain their choice.

Answers

Sample A is an example of informative writing. Acceptable responses mention that Sample A presents facts that are used to explain something to the reader, while Sample B presents opinion and unsupported statements.

Station 4

Students analyze an opinion piece from a newspaper or online news source.

Answers

Answers will vary depending upon the opinion piece provided. Accept any reasonable responses.

Materials List/Setup

Station 1	none
Station 2	none
Station 3	none
Station 4	opinion piece from a newspaper or online news source

Discussion Guide

To support students in reflecting on the activities and to gather some formative information about student learning, use the following prompts to facilitate a class discussion to "debrief" the station activities.

Prompts/Questions

1. How are narrative and informative writing different from one another?

2. What is the purpose of descriptive writing? Provide supporting examples.

3. Can descriptive writing be used in narrative, informative, and opinion writing? Explain.

4. What can you learn by analyzing an opinion piece?

Think, Pair, Share

Have students jot down their own responses to questions, then discuss with a partner (who was not in their station group), and then discuss as a whole class.

Suggested Appropriate Responses

1. Narrative writing tells a story that may, or may not, be true. Narrative writing may also include opinions. Informative writing is always based on facts, and opinions may not be shared.

2. Descriptive writing is meant to be so vivid and detailed that readers feel that they are actually living the story they are reading. Supporting examples will vary.

3. Yes, descriptive writing can be used in each of these writing strategies. It's probably more common in narratives that are written to entertain or in opinion pieces in which the writer wants to make a strong case for his or her ideas. But even informative writing can be descriptive, especially when the description makes the information easier to understand.

4. By taking the time to analyze an opinion piece, you can decide whether or not the writer is a reliable source or whether or not the opinions stated are supported by facts.

Possible Misunderstandings/Mistakes

- Confusing narrative and informative writing
- Thinking that descriptive language can only be used in narrative writing
- Confusing opinion writing with informative writing

Writing
Set 2: Types of Writing

Station 1: Narrative Writing

A **narrative** may be a true story or it can be a work of fiction. Its purpose is to tell an entertaining or interesting story. Some narratives, such as novels, are very long. But it's also possible to tell a complete story in just a few sentences.

In this activity, you will write a complete narrative using no more than 10 sentences.

Think about something important you've learned recently. It could be something you learned at school, but it could also be something you learned somewhere else. Tell the story about what you learned, but keep it very short—no more than 10 sentences. Use the space below to write your story.

_____

_____

_____

_____

_____

_____

_____

_____

_____

_____

_____

_____

_____

_____

_____

_____

_____

After you've written your story, read it to one of your group members. That person may ask questions about your story. Then your group member will read his or her story to you. Listen carefully and ask questions. When you both have had a turn to read and listen, take a few minutes to make changes in your story.

© 2011 Walch Education

Writing
Set 2: Types of Writing

Station 2: Descriptive Writing

Descriptive writing is meant to be so vivid and detailed that readers feel that they are actually living the story they are reading. Descriptive language often tells what the character is seeing, hearing, tasting, smelling, and touching. It also uses adjectives and active verbs.

At this station, you will write a description of an ordinary object. Your job is to make the description so detailed that readers can identify the object you describe without you naming it.

Here's what you need to do:

1. Think of an object you can describe in great detail without saying what the object is.

2. Think of words that describe how this object looks, sounds, smells, tastes, and feels.

3. Write a one-paragraph description of the item. Do not name the object in your paragraph, but try to make the description so clear that readers can guess what the object is.

_____
_____
_____
_____
_____
_____
_____
_____
_____
_____
_____
_____

When all your group members are finished writing, take turns reading your descriptions out loud. Group members should be able to guess each object described. After all descriptions have been read out loud, have a group discussion. Were you able to guess each mystery object? Identify the kinds of descriptive language that made it easiest to guess what object was being described. Were there objects no one was able to guess? Why? How could those descriptions be improved?

Writing
Set 2: Types of Writing

Station 3: Informative Writing

Use the activity sheet and two writing samples you find at this station to complete the station activity.

The purpose of informative writing is to share information with readers. The writer does not express an opinion about the topic—just the facts.

In this station activity, you will read two samples of writing about the same topic. One sample is an example of informative writing; the other is not. Read both writing samples and decide which one is an example of informative writing. Write your answer on the line below.

_____

Now explain your choice. Use examples from each sample to support your ideas.

_____
_____
_____
_____
_____
_____
_____
_____
_____
_____

Share your answer with your group. Did everyone choose the same sample? What reasons were given? If someone chose the other sample, what reasons were given?

continued

© 2011 Walch Education

Writing
Set 2: Types of Writing

Sample A

Beginning this fall, the school will be enforcing a new dress code. All students in grades 6–8 are now required to wear a school uniform. This uniform consists of a white shirt with a collar and khaki pants, knee-length shorts, skirt, or jumper. On cold days, students may also wear a school sweatshirt or brown coat or jacket. There are some clothing items that may never be worn at school. These items include hats of any kind, sports jackets, initial belts, and any items made out of denim.

The new dress code will be strictly enforced. Students who do not follow the dress code will be sent to the office to call their parents, who will be asked to bring a uniform to school. If a parent cannot be contacted, the office will provide a uniform that the student can wear that day.

Sample B

Have your heard about the new dress code? I have not seen the actual uniform, but it doesn't sound like something I want to wear. I suppose khaki is all right, but I don't like wearing plain, white shirts. And the school sweatshirts are really ugly. Nobody wears them. Maybe they added them to the uniform list to increase sales?

Can you imagine the office the first day of school? I'll bet that the line of kids who need to call home goes all the way to the school entrance! My parents already told me if I break the rules, I better not call them. They said I'll have to wear whatever the school gives me.

Writing
Set 2: Types of Writing

Station 4: Opinion Writing

Use the opinion piece you find at this station and this activity sheet to complete the station activity.

The purpose of opinion writing is to state an opinion. The supporting statements of an opinion piece explain the reasons the writer has for holding that opinion.

Online and print newspapers usually include an opinion or editorial section. This is where writers are able to discuss their thoughts and feelings about a topic. Read the opinion piece at this station. Then answer the questions in the chart on the next page to analyze the writing.

When you have completed the chart, discuss the following questions with your group: How did this opinion piece affect your thinking about the topic? Did it change your mind? If so, why? If not, why? Support your answers with statements from the opinion piece.

Writing
Set 2: Types of Writing

Analysis Questions	My Answers
1. What is the topic of this opinion piece?	
2. What is the writer's opinion about the topic?	
3. What approach does the writer use (for example, personal story, an important person's stand on the issue, the topic's relationship to current news)?	
4. Does the writer use humor to get points across to readers? Explain.	
5. Does the writer make any disclosures? For example, if the writer is supporting new oil drilling and works for an oil company, he or she needs to say that in the opinion piece.	

Writing

Set 3: Revising Writing

Goal: To discuss the importance of revising writing and identify strategies for editing content

Common Core Standards, Grade 6

Writing: Production and Distribution of Writing

W.6.4. Produce clear and coherent writing in which the development, organization, and style are appropriate to task, purpose, and audience.

W.6.5. With some guidance and support from peers and adults, develop and strengthen writing as needed by planning, revising, editing, rewriting, or trying a new approach.

Common Core Standards, Grade 7

Writing: Production and Distribution of Writing

W.7.4. Produce clear and coherent writing in which the development, organization, and style are appropriate to task, purpose, and audience.

W.7.5. With some guidance and support from peers and adults, develop and strengthen writing as needed by planning, revising, editing, rewriting, or trying a new approach, focusing on how well purpose and audience have been addressed.

Common Core Standards, Grade 8

Writing: Production and Distribution of Writing

W.8.4. Produce clear and coherent writing in which the development, organization, and style are appropriate to task, purpose, and audience.

W.8.5. With some guidance and support from peers and adults, develop and strengthen writing as needed by planning, revising, editing, rewriting, or trying a new approach, focusing on how well purpose and audience have been addressed.

Student Activities Overview and Answer Key

Station 1

Students review an anonymous writing sample to identify information that needs to be added for clarity.

Answers

Answers will vary depending upon the writing sample provided. Accept any reasonable responses.

Station 2

Students review an anonymous writing sample to identify information that needs to be rearranged for clarity.

Answers

Answers will vary depending upon the writing sample provided. Accept any reasonable responses.

Station 3

Students review an anonymous writing sample to identify information that needs to be removed for clarity.

Answers

Answers will vary depending upon the writing sample provided. Accept any reasonable responses.

Station 4

Students review an anonymous writing sample to identify information that needs to be replaced for clarity.

Answers

Answers will vary depending upon the writing sample provided. Accept any reasonable responses.

Materials List/Setup

Station 1   one highlighter for each group member and a class set of a sample of a former student's writing that includes few or no details

Station 2   one highlighter for each group member and a class set of a sample of a former student's writing with text that needs to be rearranged for clarity

Station 3   one highlighter for each group member and a class set of a sample of a former student's writing that includes too many details or unrelated information

Station 4   one highlighter for each group member and a class set of a sample of a former student's writing that includes text that needs to be replaced for clarity

Note: Remove student names from writing samples before duplicating.

Discussion Guide

To support students in reflecting on the activities and to gather some formative information about student learning, use the following prompts to facilitate a class discussion to "debrief" the station activities.

Prompts/Questions

1. What is the purpose of revising a piece of writing? Explain.

2. Name four strategies for revising your writing.

3. Explain the difference between adding and replacing text when you revise.

4. What questions should you ask yourself when reading to see if information needs to be removed from a text?

Think, Pair, Share

Have students jot down their own responses to questions, then discuss with a partner (who was not in their station group), and then discuss as a whole class.

Suggested Appropriate Responses

1. When you revise your writing, you are looking for ways to make it more interesting and readable. You can do this by identifying places in the text that need more, different, or less information.

2. Four strategies are adding information or details, rearranging information, removing information, and rewording information.

3. When you add information, you are including more details to make the text easier to understand. When you replace text, you are not adding more information, you are rewording the information that is already there.

4. Here are some questions you might ask: Is there a reason for including certain information or details? Is some information presented more than once? Are details repeated over and over?

Possible Misunderstandings/Mistakes

- Thinking that quantity of text is more important than its quality

- Wanting to include more information or details than are needed, then being reluctant to cut anything

- Over-using or misusing flowery language when simple descriptive statements would work as well

Writing
Set 3: Revising Writing

Station 1: Adding Information or Details

You will find a highlighter and a writing sample at this station. Use this activity sheet and the writing sample to complete this station's activity.

An important step in the writing process is revising your first draft. But it's sometimes difficult to see how to improve something you've written. The four stations in this set of activities give you four ways you can change your first drafts to make them even better. At this station, you will learn about adding information.

When you write, it's important to give readers enough information or details to be sure they understand what they are reading. But when you write about a topic that you know very well, it's easy to leave out information or details that readers need to understand the text.

The writing sample at this station is missing some very important information or details. Here is your assignment:

1. Read the sample. As you read, ask yourself what information or details are missing.

2. Use the highlighter to mark information that is unclear or incomplete.

3. When everyone in your group has finished reading, have a discussion about the sample.

4. As a group, make a list of the questions you would like to ask the writer.

_____

_____

_____

_____

_____

5. Write at least two suggestions about information or details the writer needs to add.

_____

_____

_____

_____

_____

continued

Writing
Set 3: Revising Writing

6. Think about a recent writing assignment you completed. Could you have improved your writing by adding more information or details? Explain.

_____

_____

_____

_____

_____

Writing
Set 3: Revising Writing

Station 2: Rearranging Information

You will find a highlighter and a writing sample at this station. Use this activity sheet and the writing sample to complete this station's activity.

An important step in the writing process is revising your first draft. But it's sometimes difficult to see how to improve something you've written. The four stations in this set of activities give you four ways you can change your first drafts to make them even better. At this station, you will learn about rearranging information.

During the prewriting step of the writing process, you spend time thinking about how you want to organize your ideas. However, what makes sense in a mind map or outline does not always work well when you actually begin to write. Or, organization that makes sense to you is not clear to a reader who is not familiar with your topic. In this case, you need to look at how the information is presented to see if it would make more sense if you presented it in a different order. This is called rearranging information.

The writing sample at this station includes enough information, but the information needs to be rearranged to make more sense to readers. Here is your assignment:

1. Read the sample. As you read, ask yourself how the series of events or information could be rearranged to make more sense. Also ask yourself if the writer's train of thought is clear and if the supporting details in each paragraph are related to the topic of just that paragraph. Use the highlighter to mark text that should be moved. Draw an arrow to show where you think the text should go.

2. When everyone in your group has finished reading, have a discussion about the sample.

3. As a group, describe below how you would rearrange the information in this writing sample.

_____

_____

_____

_____

_____

_____

_____

_____

_____

_____

_____

continued

Writing
Set 3: Revising Writing

4. Think about a recent writing assignment you completed. Could you have improved your writing by reorganizing the information presented? Explain.

_____

_____

_____

_____

_____

Writing
Set 3: Revising Writing

Station 3: Removing Information

You will find a highlighter and a writing sample at this station. Use this activity sheet and the writing sample to complete this station's activity.

An important step in the writing process is revising your first draft. But it's sometimes difficult to see how to improve something you've written. The four stations in this set of activities give you four ways you can change your first drafts to make them even better. At this station, you will learn about removing information.

Have you ever found yourself including more information or details than a reader needs just because you hate to leave out anything? The prewriting step helps you target just the most important information, but sometimes writers still get carried away. The problem with including too much information or detail is that your readers can become confused or bored. As hard as it may be, you sometimes need to cut some details from a first draft. This is called removing information.

The writing sample at this station includes too much information and too many details. Here is your assignment:

1. Read the sample. As you read, ask yourself the following questions: Is there a reason for including certain information or details? Is some information presented more than once, or are details repeated over and over? Use the highlighter to mark the text you think should be removed.

2. When everyone in your group has finished reading, have a discussion about the sample.

3. As a group, decide what information needs to be removed. When you come to agreement, write at least two specific suggestions below for how the writer can improve this sample by removing information.

_____

_____

_____

_____

_____

_____

_____

_____

_____

_____

continued

4. Think about a recent writing assignment you completed. Could you have improved your writing by removing information? Explain.

_____

_____

_____

_____

_____

_____

Writing
Set 3: Revising Writing

Station 4: Replacing or Rewording Information

You will find a highlighter and a writing sample at this station. Use this activity sheet and the writing sample to complete this station's activity.

An important step in the writing process is revising your first draft. But it's sometimes difficult to see how to improve something you've written. The four stations in this set of activities give you four ways you can change your first drafts to make them even better. At this station, you will learn about replacing or rewording information.

The first sentences you write may not use the best wording. It could be that a phrase or sentence doesn't sound right, is not descriptive enough, or is too wordy. Good writers read their work out loud, listening for possible problems and then making changes as needed. This is called removing or rewording information.

The writing sample at this station needs to have text replaced or reworded. Here is your assignment:

1. Read the sample out loud (softly). As you read, ask yourself: Is this easy to read out loud? Are there words and phrases that are repeated too often? Are the sentences complete? Use the highlighter to mark the text you think should be replaced or reworded.

2. When everyone in your group has finished reading, have a discussion about the sample.

3. As a group, decide what information needs to be replaced or reworded. When you come to agreement, write your changes on the writing sample.

4. Think about a recent writing assignment you completed. Could you have improved your writing by replacing or rewording information? Explain.

_____

_____

_____

_____

_____

Writing

Instruction

Goal: To identify and analyze suitable references and informational resources for a variety of purposes

Common Core Standards, Grade 6

Writing: Research to Build and Present Knowledge

W.6.8. Gather relevant information from multiple print and digital sources; assess the credibility of each source; and quote or paraphrase the data and conclusions of others while avoiding plagiarism and providing basic bibliographic information for sources.

W.6.9. Draw evidence from literary or informational texts to support analysis, reflection, and research.

Common Core Standards, Grade 7

Writing: Research to Build and Present Knowledge

W.7.8. Gather relevant information from multiple print and digital sources, using search terms effectively; assess the credibility and accuracy of each source; and quote or paraphrase the data and conclusions of others while avoiding plagiarism and following a standard format for citation.

W.7.9. Draw evidence from literary or informational texts to support analysis, reflection, and research.

Common Core Standards, Grade 8

Writing: Research to Build and Present Knowledge

W.8.8. Gather relevant information from multiple print and digital sources, using search terms effectively; assess the credibility and accuracy of each source; and quote or paraphrase the data and conclusions of others while avoiding plagiarism and following a standard format for citation.

W.8.9. Draw evidence from literary or informational texts to support analysis, reflection, and research.

Student Activities Overview and Answer Key
Station 1

Students explain the purpose for various reference materials.

Answers

Answers may vary, but acceptable responses may include:

1. dictionary—a book that contains an alphabetical list of words
   You use a dictionary to find out how to spell a word, what the word means, how to pronounce the word, and the origins of the word.

2. thesaurus—a book of synonyms and sometimes antonyms for words
   Use a thesaurus when you want to use or improve descriptive language.

3. encyclopedia—a book or set of books that consists of informational articles arranged in alphabetical order
   Use an encyclopedia when starting your research to get general information about a topic.

4. atlas—a collection of maps
   Use an atlas when you are writing a research paper for a social studies class.

5. grammar and style guide—a collection of rules of grammar and guidelines for writing research papers
   Use a grammar and style guide whenever you write a research paper.

6. almanac—a yearly publication that includes weather forecasts and other information arranged by date
   An almanac might be helpful for a science research paper.

Station 2

Students evaluate an online reference site.

Answers

Answers will vary. Accept any reasonable responses.

Station 3

Students practice documenting informational resources.

Answers

Answers will vary depending upon reference materials provided. Accept responses in which students correctly identify information.

Station 4

Students create a sample six-entry bibliography.

Answers

Answers will vary depending upon reference materials provided. Accept responses in which students correctly format citations in proper alphabetical order.

Materials List/Setup

Station 1   none

Station 2   Internet-connected computers (one for each student at the station) with several Web sites bookmarked for students to review

Station 3   assorted reference materials (include at least one each of the following: book; encyclopedia volume; magazine, newspaper, or journal article; video or film; printout of Web site home page)

Station 4   assorted reference materials (include at least one of each of the following: book; encyclopedia volume; magazine, newspaper, or journal article; printout of Web site home page)

Discussion Guide

To support students in reflecting on the activities and to gather some formative information about student learning, use the following prompts to facilitate a class discussion to "debrief" the station activities.

Prompts/Questions

1. Explain why you need to use several types of reference materials when doing research.

2. Why should you take the time to evaluate a Web site before citing it in a bibliography?

3. Describe how documenting references fits into the research process.

4. How is writing a bibliography different from documenting references?

Think, Pair, Share

Have students jot down their own responses to questions, then discuss with a partner (who was not in their station group), and then discuss as a whole class.

Suggested Appropriate Responses

1. Different types of reference materials provide different kinds of information. For example, you can find general information in an encyclopedia article and then get more specific information in a book or magazine article.

2. Anyone can post a Web site that appears to be reliable. By taking the time to review the site, you can decide whether or not it is a trusted source.

3. When you do careful research, you will look at many different reference materials. By the time you're done researching, you may forget where you found information you want to use. By documenting references and taking notes, you will easily locate your sources when it's time to write.

4. When you document references, you need to note important information, but there's no set format, and the references don't need to be listed alphabetically. When writing a bibliography, references need to be cited using a special format and listed alphabetically. Also, you only list references in a bibliography when you actually used the information in your paper.

Possible Misunderstandings/Mistakes

- Not understanding the purpose of using multiple reference materials
- Thinking that documenting references is a waste of time
- Forgetting to use the proper citation formats for various reference materials

Writing
Set 4: Using Reference Materials

Station 1: Using a Variety of Resources

When writing a research report, the first step in the process is to identify the key ideas in the topic. After that, you work out when you need to have each step done. Then you begin the actual research.

There are many different reference materials, and, in most cases, you need to use several types to do your research. You can save a lot of time if you think about the different types of resources available to you and the types of information you can find in them. For example, if you are working on research for a social studies class, you would not take time to look at math reference tables.

Below is a list of six common reference materials. Write a description for as many as you know. Include the kind of information you would find in each resource and when you might need to use it.

1. dictionary _____

_____

_____

2. thesaurus _____

_____

_____

3. encyclopedia _____

_____

_____

4. atlas _____

_____

_____

5. grammar and style guide _____

_____

_____

6. almanac _____

_____

_____

Once you've written as many descriptions as you know, work collaboratively with other team members to complete the missing descriptions.

Writing
Set 4: Using Reference Materials

Station 2: Evaluating Online Reference Sites

You will need a computer with Internet access to complete this station activity.

The Internet is a good place to find reference materials. But before you use an online resource, you need to check to be sure that the information posted there is accurate and comes from a source you can trust.

Use the following chart to evaluate one of the online references your teacher has bookmarked for you to review.

Web Site Evaluation Checklist		
Name of Web site:		
Web site address:		
Owner/Author:		
Is the Web site . . .	Yes	No
User friendly? Are pages easy to read and navigate?		
Up to date, with links to recent information and few broken links?		
Is the information . . .		
From a trusted source?		
Accurate?		
Useful?		
Comments:		

Discuss your answers with your group members. Were there questions you could not answer? How did other group members respond to those same questions?

Writing
Set 4: Using Reference Materials

Station 3: Documenting Informational Resources

You will find a collection of reference materials at this station. Use these materials to complete the activity.

As a writer, you must be able to support statements you make by referring to the information sources used during your research. How do you keep track of the resources you review?

One simple strategy is to use index cards to record basic information about the reference and your notes about the information. At this station, you will practice finding basic information about several different types of reference materials.

Complete the chart on the next page using the reference materials found at this station.

continued

Writing
Set 4: Using Reference Materials

Book	
Author (or authors, if more than one)	
Title (underlined)	
Place of publication	
Publisher	
Copyright date	
Encyclopedia	
Author (if given)	
Title of article (in quotation marks)	
Name of encyclopedia (underlined)	
Edition (year)	
Volume number	
Magazine, newspaper, or journal article	
Author of article	
Title of article (in quotation marks)	
Name of magazine (underlined)	
Volume number	
Date	
Page	
Video or film	
Title (underlined)	
Director	
Distributor	
Year released	
Internet	
Author's name (if available)	
Title of document	
Source organization (if available)	
<URL> (between angle brackets)	
Date accessed	

Writing
Set 4: Using Reference Materials

Station 4: Bibliography Citations

You will find a collection of reference materials at this station. Use these materials to complete the activity.

A **bibliography** is an alphabetized list of reference materials used by a writer while doing research. Each listing in a bibliography is called a **citation**.

Bibliographic citations are written in special formats. Use the reference materials at this station and the model formats provided below to create a six-entry sample bibliography. Remember to alphabetize the citations. Capitalize author names, publication titles, article titles, city where the item was published, and publisher.

Book, one author

Author (last name, first name). Title of book. City: Publisher, date of publication.

Book, two authors

Author (last name, first name) and second author (first name and last name). Title of book. City: Publisher, date of publication.

Book, no author named

Title. City: Publisher, date of publication.

Encyclopedia

Author of Article (if given). "Article Title." Encyclopedia title, Edition date.

Magazine Article

Author (last name, first name). "Article Title." Name of Magazine. Date: Page(s).

Newspaper Article

Author (last name, first name). "Article Title." Name of newspaper. Date: Edition (if available), Section, Page(s).

Web Site

Creator's name (if given), last name first. Web page title. Date of latest update. Institution or organization. Date of access, <URL network address>.

When you finish your sample bibliography, exchange papers with another group member and proofread his or her bibliography. Look for mistakes in formatting and alphabetizing.

Language

Goal: To provide opportunities for students to identify, analyze, and apply knowledge of figurative language, including metonymy, hyperbole, metaphor, and simile

Common Core Standards, Grade 6

Language: Vocabulary Acquisition and Use

L.6.5.   Demonstrate understanding of figurative language, word relationships, and nuances in word meanings.

   a. Interpret figures of speech (e.g., personification) in context.

Common Core Standards, Grade 7

Language: Vocabulary Acquisition and Use

L.7.5.   Demonstrate understanding of figurative language, word relationships, and nuances in word meanings.

   a. Interpret figures of speech (e.g., literary, biblical, and mythological allusions) in context.

Common Core Standards, Grade 8

Language: Vocabulary Acquisition and Use

L.8.5.   Demonstrate understanding of figurative language, word relationships, and nuances in word meanings.

   a. Interpret figures of speech (e.g., verbal irony, puns) in context.

Student Activities Overview and Answer Key
Station 1

Students practice their skills at recognizing metonymy.

Answers

Rewritten sentences may vary somewhat, but answers should be similar to the following:
1. The entrée was served after the salad.

2. Finishing the job on time will not be difficult.

3. A photo of the fiery wreck was printed in the newspaper.

4. Yesterday the royal family announced the birth of a princess.

5. Officers from Scotland Yard have arrested a suspect in the recent bank robbery.

Station 2

Students demonstrate their ability to recognize examples of hyperbole in print advertisements.

Answers

Answers will vary depending upon the advertisements selected. Accept any reasonable responses.

Station 3

Students use a metaphor to write a self-description.

Answers

Answers will vary depending upon the individual student. Accept any reasonable responses.

Station 4

Students write similes for five topics.

Answers

Answers will vary. Accept any reasonable responses.

Materials List/Setup

Station 1	none
Station 2	three print advertisements that use hyperbole
Station 3	none
Station 4	none

Discussion Guide

To support students in reflecting on the activities and to gather some formative information about student learning, use the following prompts to facilitate a class discussion to "debrief" the station activities.

Prompts/Questions

1. Organize the four figures of speech covered in these station activities into a list, with the first being the easiest to recognize or write and fourth being most difficult to recognize or write. Explain your answer.

2. Compare and contrast similes and metaphors.

3. Analyze how understanding more about figures of speech helps you when you read.

4. Analyze how understanding more about figures of speech helps you when you write.

Think, Pair, Share

Have students jot down their own responses to questions, then discuss with a partner (who was not in their station group), and then discuss as a whole class.

Suggested Appropriate Responses

1. Answers will vary.

2. Both compare items that are usually unlike. Similes include use of the word *like* or *as*, but metaphors do not.

3. Answers will vary, but should mention that it's important to understand that figures of speech do not literally mean what they say.

4. Answers will vary, but should mention that use of figures of speech can make writing more descriptive and interesting.

Possible Misunderstandings/Mistakes

- Confusing similes with metaphors
- Inability to identify incorrect terms in examples of metonymy
- Accepting exaggerations in hyperbole as truth

English Language Arts Station Activities for Common Core State Standards

© 2011 Walch Education

Language
Set 1: Figurative Language

Station 1: Metonymy

Metonymy is a figure of speech in which one word or phrase is used in place of another word or phrase that is closely associated. For example, people often say "Washington" when they are talking about the U.S. government.

Here are a few examples:

- *Ted watered the lawn.* Did water actually spout from Ted, or did he use a hose?

- *She has brains.* Does this person actually have brains that she's holding, or is she very smart?

- *The laundry ironed Dad's shirts.* Did the business iron the shirts, or were they ironed by someone who works at the laundry?

The examples above could be rewritten in the following ways:

- Ted used a hose to water the lawn.

- She is smart.

- A clerk at the laundry ironed Dad's shirts.

As you can see, metonymy can be tricky because we don't usually think about the fact that an incorrect term is being used. Now read the following examples of metonymy. Rewrite each example so that the proper term is used.

1. The main dish was served after the salad. _____

   _____

2. Finishing the job on time will be no sweat. _____

   _____

3. The press released a photo of the fiery wreck. _____

   _____

4. Yesterday the palace announced the birth of a princess. _____

   _____

5. Scotland Yard has arrested a suspect in the recent bank robbery. _____

   _____

Compare your answers with those of another group member. How are they alike? How are they different? Is there just one right way to rewrite each sentence?

Language
Set 1: Figurative Language

Station 2: Hyperbole

At this station, you will find three print advertisements. Use them to identify examples of hyperbole.

Hyperbole is an extremely exaggerated overstatement. Advertisements can be examples of hyperbole when they make exaggerated claims. For example, some ads claim that using a certain product will make a person's dreams come true or change their lives in some other way.

Look at the advertisements at this station. Answer the following questions to see how hyperbole is used in each one.

Advertisement 1

1. Describe the situation shown in the advertisement.

_____

_____

_____

2. What element of the situation is being exaggerated?

_____

_____

_____

3. What is the hyperbole in this advertisement?

_____

_____

_____

Advertisement 2

1. Describe the situation shown in the advertisement.

_____

_____

_____

continued

2. What element of the situation is being exaggerated?

_____

_____

_____

3. What is the hyperbole in this advertisement?

_____

_____

_____

Advertisement 3

1. Describe the situation shown in the advertisement.

_____

_____

_____

2. What element of the situation is being exaggerated?

_____

_____

_____

3. What is the hyperbole in this advertisement?

_____

_____

_____

When you finish, compare your answers with your group members' answers. Are your answers alike or different? Do you want to change any of your original answers?

Language
Set 1: Figurative Language

Station 3: Metaphor

Use this activity sheet to practice your skill at writing a metaphor. Do not write your name on the activity sheet yet.

A **metaphor** compares two items that are not alike. However, a metaphor does not use the connector *like* or *as*. It makes a direct comparison.

Here are a few examples:

- He has the heart of a lion.
- She is the life of the party.
- The baby's sunny character makes her easy to care for.

1. The examples above all compare people to unlike items. Think about yourself. If you were compared to an unlike item, what would it be?

   _____

   _____

2. Now think about three special qualities about that item that you might use in a metaphor. List them here.

   _____

   _____

3. Now write a three- or four-sentence metaphor comparing yourself to the unlike item you chose.

   _____

   _____

   _____

   _____

   _____

When every group member is finished, shuffle the activity sheets and take turns reading the metaphor out loud. Can you guess who wrote each one? Discuss your guesses. Write your name on your activity sheet before you turn it in.

Language
Set 1: Figurative Language

Station 4: Similes

A **simile** is a figure of speech in which two elements are compared by using the word *like* or the word *as*. Whenever you are reading a colorful or vivid description and the word *like* or *as* is used, it is almost always a simile.

Here are a few examples:

- Darkness covered the neighborhood like a cloak.
- The long-distance runner was as tall as a pole and as skinny as a rail.
- Waiting for the plane to arrive was as painful as a toothache.

Now it's your turn. Write a simile that describes each of the following topics.

1. a class you enjoy _____
   _____

2. the best meal you've ever eaten_____
   _____

3. something that scares you _____
   _____

4. your favorite musical performer _____
   _____

5. an annoying celebrity _____
   _____

Share your similes with your group members. Discuss the different responses for each topic and choose the one you like best for each topic.

English Language Arts Station Activities for Common Core State Standards

Language

Goal: To discuss the importance of revising writing and identify strategies for editing content

Common Core Standards, Grade 6

Language: Conventions of Standard English

L.6.1. Demonstrate command of the conventions of standard English grammar and usage when writing or speaking.

   a. Ensure that pronouns are in the proper case (subjective, objective, possessive).

   c. Recognize and correct inappropriate shifts in pronoun number and person.*

   d. Recognize and correct vague pronouns (i.e., ones with unclear or ambiguous antecedents).*

   e. Recognize variations from standard English in their own and others' writing and speaking, and identify and use strategies to improve expression in conventional language.*

Language: Knowledge of Language

L.6.3. Use knowledge of language and its conventions when writing, speaking, reading, or listening.

Common Core Standards, Grade 7

Language: Conventions of Standard English

L.7.1. Demonstrate command of the conventions of standard English grammar and usage when writing or speaking.

Language: Knowledge of Language

L.7.3. Use knowledge of language and its conventions when writing, speaking, reading, or listening.

Common Core Standards, Grade 8

Language: Conventions of Standard English

L.8.1. Demonstrate command of the conventions of standard English grammar and usage when writing or speaking.

   d. Recognize and correct inappropriate shifts in verb voice and mood.*

*Denotes standards requiring continued attention in higher grades

Student Activities Overview and Answer Key

Station 1

Students complete a chart of proofreading symbols and abbreviations.

Answers

Example
Our class ended early today⊙
The cafeteria served salad ∧ lunch.   for
The phone rang rang twice.
"Please stop texting me," she said. ∧ "Okay," I replied.
Let's try ⌐assignment ⌐this⌐ again.
My homework is nearly done ⊙

Meaning
awkward wording
capitalize
fragment
spelling
wordy

Station 2

Students review three common grammatical errors: misrelated modifiers, shift in person, and shift in tense.

Answers

Mistake—Misrelated Modifiers

1. The principal was knocked over by a student who was racing to beat the bell.

2. I ate the chocolate chip cookies that Mom left on the plate.

3. I rode my bike with a broken handlebar to the park.

Mistake—Shift in Person

The new school was much bigger than ~~I~~ *you* imagined. ~~I~~ *You* saw students walking in and out of at least four different buildings. ~~I~~ *You* finally found what ~~I~~ *you* hoped was the main building. When ~~I~~ *you* got to the office, the first thing the secretary handed ~~me~~ *you* was a map. "Study this tonight," she said.

Mistake—Shift in Tense

I saw the baby crawl near the electric heater. At first I thought she would stop, but then I saw that she kept going. "No, Baby!" I shouted. "Don't touch the heater!"

Station 3

Students review three common grammatical errors: pronoun reference, pronoun/antecedent agreement, and subject/verb agreement.

Answers

Mistake—Pronoun Reference

1. Once again, my parents have changed the rules.

2. Your key will be easier to find later if you leave it on the table.

3. It's good that I'm almost finished with this book.

Mistake—Pronoun/Antecedent Agreement

1. Everybody needs to give his or her time for this project.

2. If either of the boys is chosen for the team, he will fit into the extra uniform.

3. Three fathers volunteered their time to supervise the game.

Mistake—Subject/Verb Agreement

1. Each of the students knows what to do.

2. Measles is a dangerous disease.

3. He doesn't like getting up in the morning.

Station 4

Students review samples of their own writing to identify their common errors.

Answers

Answers will vary for each student. Accept any reasonable responses.

Materials List/Setup

Station 1   none

Station 2   none

Station 3   none

Station 4   2 to 3 short samples of each student's own writing from past assignments

Discussion Guide

To support students in reflecting on the activities and to gather some formative information about student learning, use the following prompts to facilitate a class discussion to "debrief" the station activities.

Prompts/Questions

1. How is proofreading different from revising? Explain.

2. What is a "shift in tense"? Why should writers avoid doing this?

3. Explain the term *pronoun/antecedent agreement*.

4. Name three reading strategies for proofreading your own work. Why read your writing more than once?

Think, Pair, Share

Have students jot down their own responses to questions, then discuss with a partner (who was not in their station group), and then discuss as a whole class.

Suggested Appropriate Responses

1. When you revise your writing, you are looking for ways to make it more interesting and readable. When you proofread, you are looking for mistakes in spelling, grammar, and punctuation.

2. Writers need to decide early in the writing process what verb tense they will use. Once chosen, if the writer decides to use a different tense, he or she has "shifted tense." This is acceptable occasionally, but should not happen regularly because it confuses readers.

3. A pronoun can be used in place of a noun. If the noun (also called the antecedent) is singular, the pronoun must be singular. If the antecedent is plural, the pronoun must also be plural. This is also referred to as "being in agreement."

4. Read the writing silently, read it out loud, read it from last sentence to first. Rereading the work in different ways helps the writer find all his/her mistakes.

Possible Misunderstandings/Mistakes

- Not using standard symbols and abbreviations for proofreading personal work
- Forgetting that words such as *everyone* or *anybody* are singular, not plural
- Thinking that it's possible to find all mistakes in one quick review of a document

Language
Set 2: Proofreading

Station 1: Proofreading Symbols and Abbreviations

In addition to improving the quality of your writing by revising, it's also important to correct mistakes in grammar, spelling, and punctuation. This is called **proofreading**.

When you proofread, there is a standard set of symbols and abbreviations for you to use as you identify mistakes. This makes it possible for anyone who reads the proofreading marks to understand exactly what you meant.

On the next page, you'll find a chart of proofreading symbols and abbreviations, but it is missing some information. Follow the directions to complete the chart on your own. Then discuss your answers with your group. After the discussion, make changes in your answers, if needed.

Once the chart is finished, you can use it as a guide to proofread your future work.

continued

Language
Set 2: Proofreading

Proofreading Symbols and Abbreviations		

Complete each example by adding the missing proofreading symbol in the "Example" column.

Symbol	Meaning	Example
∧	Insert something.	The cafeteria served salad lunch.
⊙	Add a period here.	Our class ended early today
ℓ	Delete this.	The phone rang rang twice.
¶	Begin new paragraph.	"Please stop texting me," she said. "Okay," I replied.
⌐⌐⌐	Transpose something.	Let's try assignment this again.
◡	Close this space.	My work is nearly done .

Proofreading abbreviations are written in the margin to point out mistakes. Read each abbreviation and its example. Using this information, write the meaning for each abbreviation in the column labeled "Meaning." The first meaning is added for you.

Abbreviation	Meaning	Example
awk	awkward wording	*awk* The poem had the effect of making me happy and sad at the same time.
cap		I like the song about rain in spain. *cap*
frag		*frag* As soon as my work is finished and after I have a snack.
sp		*sp* (Skool) begins soon.
wdy		Seldom have I eaten a *wdy* sandwich so tasty, consisting of extraordinarily delicious bread with an exquisitely fresh homemade filling.

Language
Set 2: Proofreading

Station 2: Identifying Common Grammar Mistakes I

Even though every writer is unique, there are some mistakes that nearly every writer makes at one time or another. At this station, you will practice recognizing three of these common mistakes.

Mistake—Misrelated Modifiers

A modifier is one or more words that describe or limit another word or group of words. Sometimes writers put a modifier in the wrong place in a sentence. Look at this example:

> Lisa saw a car jump the curb <u>while walking to the store</u>.

The modifier is the underlined phrase, but was Lisa walking to the store or was the car walking to the store? To make the sentence clear, rewrite it like this:

> <u>While walking to the store</u>, Lisa saw a car jump the curb.

Now it's clear that the modifier describes what Lisa was doing.

Now it's your turn. Rewrite each sentence so the modifier is in the correct place.

1. While racing to beat the bell, the principal was knocked over by a student.

    _____

    _____

2. Mom left chocolate chip cookies on the plate, which I ate. _____

    _____

3. I rode my bike to the park with a broken handlebar. _____

    _____

Mistake—Shift in Person

A pronoun refers back to a noun or takes the place of that noun. It's important to use pronouns correctly so your readers know which noun your pronoun refers to. Writers often confuse readers by switching from first-person pronouns (*I* or *me*) to second person (*you*). Look at this example:

> <u>I</u> have a new laptop that's the latest model <u>you</u> could buy.

continued

The underlined pronouns show a shift in person. The writer probably means that the laptop was the newest model *she* could buy, not the reader. To make the sentence clear, rewrite it like this:

I have a new laptop that's the latest model I could buy.

Now it's your turn. This paragraph is written in first person. Cross out all the first-person pronouns and replace them with second-person pronouns.

The new school was much bigger than I imagined. I saw students walking in and out

of at least four different buildings. I finally found what I hoped was the main building.

When I got to the office, the first thing the secretary handed me was a map. "Study

this tonight," she said.

Mistake—Shift in Tense

The tense of a verb tells you if something happened in the past, is happening now in the present, or will happen in the future. When you write, it's important to choose the tense you plan to use and then stick with it, unless there is a very good reason for shifting. Read the following example:

I <u>went</u> shopping last night. The salesgirl <u>comes</u> up to me and <u>asks</u> what I <u>want</u>. But she <u>looks</u> like she <u>wishes</u> I would just leave.

The underlined words are all verbs. The first verb is in the past tense, but the other verbs are all in the present tense. This is a case of shift in tense. To make the sentences clear, rewrite them like this:

I <u>went</u> shopping last night. The salesgirl <u>came</u> up to me and <u>asked</u> what I <u>wanted</u>. But she <u>looked</u> like she <u>wished</u> I would just leave.

Now it's your turn. Edit this paragraph so there are no shifts in tense:

I see the baby crawled near the electric heater. At first I'm thinking she stopped, but

then I saw that she was still going. "No, Baby!" I shout. "Don't touch the heater!"

_____

_____

_____

Discuss your answers to this station's activities with your group members. Which type of mistake was easiest for you to recognize and correct? Which was most difficult?

Language
Set 2: Proofreading

Station 3: Identifying Common Grammar Mistakes II

Even though every writer is unique, there are some mistakes that nearly every writer makes at one time or another. At this station, you will practice recognizing three of these common mistakes.

Mistake—Pronoun Reference

A pronoun refers back to a noun or takes the place of that noun. To avoid confusion, writers need to make sure that the pronoun used refers clearly to a specific noun. For example:

> The <u>car bumper</u> nicked the <u>dog's leg</u>, but <u>it</u> wasn't damaged.

Is "it" the car bumper or the dog's leg? The sentence can be rewritten like this:

> Although <u>it</u> was nicked by the car's bumper, the <u>dog's leg</u> wasn't damaged.

Now it's your turn. Rewrite each sentence so that the pronoun used clearly refers to a specific noun. The questions in parentheses provide hints.

1. Once again, they've changed the rules. (Who is "they"?)

   _____

2. If you leave your key on the table, you can find it later. (What will be easy to find, the key or the table?)

   _____

3. I'm almost finished with this book, which is good. (What is good, finishing the book or the book itself?)

   _____

Mistake—Pronoun/Antecedent Agreement

A pronoun refers back to a noun or takes the place of that noun. If the noun (also called the antecedent) is singular, the pronoun must be singular. If the antecedent is plural, the pronoun must also be plural. Look at this example:

> Next week my school will host a <u>dance</u>. <u>These</u> will help pay for new library books.

The antecedent and pronoun, which are underlined, are not in agreement because "dance" is singular and "these" is plural. The sentences can be rewritten like this:

> Next week my school is hosting a <u>dance</u>. <u>This</u> will help pay for new library books.

continued

Language
Set 2: Proofreading

Now it's your turn. Rewrite the sentences below so that the pronouns and antecedents are in agreement.

1. Everybody needs to give their time for this project. _____

   _____

2. If either of the boys is chosen for the team, they will fit into the extra uniform.

   _____

   _____

3. Three fathers volunteered his time to supervise the game. _____

   _____

Mistake—Subject/Verb Agreement

Singular means one and *plural* means more than one. When writing a sentence, if you have a singular subject, you must use a singular verb. If you have a plural subject, you must use a plural verb. It sounds easy, but writers often make the simple mistake of using subjects and verbs that do not agree. Look at this example:

The <u>books</u> from the library <u>looks</u> interesting.

The subject of this sentence is "books," not "library." So the verb "looks" needs to agree with the subject "books." The correct way to write the sentence is:

The <u>books</u> from the library <u>look</u> interesting.

Now it's your turn. Rewrite each sentence below so the subject and verb are in agreement.

1. Each of the students know what to do. _____

   _____

2. Measles are a dangerous disease. _____

   _____

3. He don't like getting up in the morning. _____

   _____

Discuss your answers with your group members. Which type of mistake in this station's activities was easiest for you to recognize and correct? Which was most difficult?

Language
Set 2: Proofreading

Station 4: Identifying Your Common Mistakes

Use the 2 to 3 short writing samples your teacher gave you to complete this station's activity.

When you proofread, you read a document to find mistakes in spelling, grammar, and punctuation. One of the best strategies for proofreading your own work is to become familiar with the mistakes you commonly make. This activity is designed to help you identify your common mistakes.

Reading your work more than once, using a different strategy each time, will help you find most or all of your mistakes. Start by simply reading the samples of your own work that your teacher provides. Now read them again, but this time, read the samples out loud (softly). Finally, read the samples again sentence by sentence, from the last sentence to the first sentence.

Use the chart on the next page to write a summary of the common mistakes you made in your writing samples.

When you complete your chart, have a discussion with your group. Use these questions to get started: What did you learn from this activity? How can you use this information for future writing assignments?

continued

My Common Mistakes
Use this chart to write a summary of the common mistakes you made in your writing samples. Include comments for each area listed.
Spelling:
Punctuation:
Verbs:
Subject/verb agreement:
Pronouns:
Other mistakes:

© 2011 Walch Education

English Language Arts Station Activities for Common Core State Standards

Language

Set 3: Parts of Speech—Nouns and Pronouns

Goal: To recognize and analyze nouns and pronouns, including form, spelling, and what these words do in a sentence

Common Core Standards, Grade 6

Language: Conventions of Standard English

L.6.1. Demonstrate command of the conventions of standard English grammar and usage when writing or speaking.

   a. Ensure that pronouns are in the proper case (subjective, objective, possessive).

   c. Recognize and correct inappropriate shifts in pronoun number and person.*

   d. Recognize and correct vague pronouns (i.e., ones with unclear or ambiguous antecedents).*

   e. Recognize variations from standard English in their own and others' writing and speaking, and identify and use strategies to improve expression in conventional language.*

Student Activities Overview and Answer Key
Station 1

Students identify the correct spelling of possessive nouns.

Answers

1.	Julio's	6.	children's
2.	elephants'	7.	geese's
3.	baby's	8.	men's
4.	Street's	9.	alumni's
5.	Smiths'	10.	oxen's

Answers about preferred possessive form will vary.

Station 2

Students identify the subject, direct object, and indirect object in sentences. Students will mark the subject of each sentence yellow, the direct object pink, and the indirect object blue. Here, subjects are underlined; direct objects are circled; and indirect objects are in boxes.

*Denotes standards requiring continued attention in higher grades

Language
Set 3: Parts of Speech—Nouns and Pronouns

Answers

1. Pedro willingly gave his [sister] a (loan.)

2. The Smiths gave [Shelley] a birthday (party.)

3. Molly sent [Dave] an (e-mail.)

4. The teachers gave the [students] an extra (break.)

5. My mom told [me] a (story)

Student-written sentences will vary. Accept all sentences that include a subject, a direct object, and an indirect object.

Station 3

Students practice using interrogative and relative pronouns.

Answers

Answers will vary. Accept responses in which students properly use interrogative and relative pronouns.

Station 4

Students proofread sentences in which indefinite pronouns are used.

Answers

1. his or her
2. correct
3. they
4. falls

5. know
6. his or her
7. correct
8. was

Group sentences will vary. Accept responses that make correct use of indefinite pronouns.

Materials List/Setup

Station 1   none

Station 2   sets of highlighters (yellow, pink, and blue in each set—one for each student at this station)

Station 3   none

Station 4   none

Language
Set 3: Parts of Speech—Nouns and Pronouns

Discussion Guide

To support students in reflecting on the activities and to gather some formative information about student learning, use the following prompts to facilitate a class discussion to "debrief" the station activities.

Prompts/Questions

1. When a singular noun ends with an *s*, how do you make it possessive?

2. What is the difference between a direct object and an indirect object? Explain.

3. Define the term *interrogative pronoun* and give an example of one.

4. What common mistake is made when a writer uses a singular indefinite pronoun? Give an example.

Think, Pair, Share

Have students jot down their own responses to questions, then discuss with a partner (who was not in their station group), and then discuss as a whole class.

Suggested Appropriate Responses

1. There are two ways to make a singular noun that ends with an *s* possessive. You can just add an apostrophe or you can add an apostrophe and an *s*.

2. A direct object is a noun that follows an action verb and answers the question "who?" or "what?" about the verb. An indirect object is a noun that follows an action verb that tells us to whom or to what something was done. An indirect object is always located between an action verb and a direct object.

3. An interrogative pronoun is a pronoun used to ask a question: what, which, who, whom, or whose.

4. A common mistake is to use a plural pronoun with an indefinite pronoun. For example, "Everyone needs their own space," instead of "Everyone needs his or her own space."

Possible Misunderstandings/Mistakes

*   Improper placement of the apostrophe when making a noun possessive
*   Thinking that an indirect object can come after a direct object in a sentence
*   Forgetting that indefinite pronouns such as *everybody* or *someone* are singular, not plural

Language
Set 3: Parts of Speech—Nouns and Pronouns

Station 1: Possessive Nouns

A **possessive noun** shows ownership of something by a person, place, or thing. Possessive nouns can be singular (one owner) or plural (more than one owner). Singular ownership is shown by adding *'s*. Plural ownership is shown by adding *s'*.

This seems simple, but it's very common to see possessive nouns that are not written correctly. This station activity provides practice in recognizing correctly written possessive nouns.

Circle the correct possessive noun in each sentence.

1. (Julio's, Julios') dad picked him up after the game.

2. The (elephant's, elephants') trunks were swinging as they walked in the parade.

3. The (baby's, babies') diaper needs to be changed.

4. Main (Street's, Streets') stores are the best in town!

5. The (Smith's, Smiths') car broke down last week.

There are exceptions to the rule. For example, when the plural form of a noun is irregular, you need to add *'s* to make the plural noun possessive. So, the possessive form of *women* is *women's*.

How would you write the plural possessive form of these irregular nouns?

6. children _____

7. geese _____

8. men _____

9. alumni _____

10. oxen _____

Not everyone agrees on the proper possessive form for a singular noun that ends with the letter *s*. Should you write *Charles'* or *Charles's*? Both are correct. The most important thing is to choose one of the two and then use the same form throughout the document. Which form do you prefer to use? Explain your answer here.

_____

_____

_____

When you finish, compare your answers with other group members' answers. If you disagree, discuss the answers and try to reach an agreement.

Language
Set 3: Parts of Speech—Nouns and Pronouns

Station 2: Subjects, Direct Objects, and Indirect Objects

You will find sets of highlighters (yellow, pink, and blue in each set) at this station. Use the highlighters to complete the station activity.

Nouns can do several different jobs in a sentence. Three of these jobs are:

- **subject of a sentence**—what or whom the sentence is about
- **direct object**—a noun that follows an action verb and answers the question "who?" or "what?" about the verb
- **indirect object**—a noun that follows an action verb that tells us to whom or to what something was done; always located between an action verb and a direct object

Each of these sentences includes a subject, a direct object, and an indirect object. Mark the subject of each sentence yellow, the direct object pink, and the indirect object blue.

1. Pedro willingly gave his sister a loan.

2. The Smiths gave Shelley a birthday party.

3. Molly sent Dave an e-mail.

4. The teachers gave the students an extra break.

5. My mom told me a story.

Now it's your turn. Write three sentences that each include a subject, a direct object, and an indirect object.

_____

_____

_____

Exchange your paper with the paper of another group member. Read the sentences he or she wrote and use the highlighters to mark the subject (yellow), direct object (pink), and indirect object (blue) in each. If you cannot find one or more of these nouns in a sentence, check with the group member who wrote the sentence.

Language
Set 3: Parts of Speech—Nouns and Pronouns

Station 3: Interrogative Pronouns

An **interrogative pronoun** is a pronoun used to ask a question. All the words in the box below are interrogative pronouns.

what	whom
which	whose
who	

Writers are sometimes confused about when to use *who* and when to use *whom*. Just remember that *who* = subject and *whom* = object.

Write five questions. Use a different interrogative pronoun in each question.

_____

_____

_____

_____

_____

Some interrogative pronouns can also be relative pronouns. A **relative pronoun** relates to another noun that comes before it in a sentence. Example: The <u>teacher who</u> won the award is my aunt.

The box below contains relative pronouns.

who	whom
whoever	whomever
which	

Write five sentences that use a different relative pronoun in each.

_____

_____

_____

_____

_____

When you are finished, exchange your paper with the paper of another group member and read the sentences he or she wrote. Are the interrogative and relative pronouns used properly? Do you have suggestions for improving any of the sentences? Do you have any questions about the sentences? Discuss your thoughts and suggestions with this person.

Language
Set 3: Parts of Speech—Nouns and Pronouns

Station 4: Indefinite Pronouns

Indefinite pronouns refer to an undefined or unknown person, place, or thing. Most indefinite pronouns are singular. Here is a list of singular indefinite pronouns:

another	anyone	anybody
anything	everyone	everybody
everything	nothing	each
either	no one	neither
nobody	one	someone
somebody	something	

A few indefinite pronouns are plural. Below is a list of plural indefinite pronouns.

both	few
many	several

Each sentence below includes an indefinite pronoun. Proofread the sentences to be sure that any verbs or personal pronouns used are in agreement. If the sentence is correct, do nothing. If there is a mistake, cross out the incorrect verb or pronoun and write the correct verb or pronoun at the end of the sentence.

1. Everyone wants to have their fair share of the prize.

2. No one was able to get the cat out of the tree.

3. Many think he or she will get A's on the test.

4. Everything fall off the shelf during an earthquake.

5. Few knows that I was born in Ohio.

6. Anyone is able to turn in their contest entry.

7. Somebody left his or her backpack in the classroom.

8. Nothing were done when Anna arrived.

When you finish proofreading the sentences, collaborate with your group to correctly write three sentences that use indefinite pronouns.

_____

_____

_____

Language

Instruction

Goal: To recognize, analyze, and write sentences

Common Core Standards, Grade 6

Language: Conventions of Standard English

L.6.2. Demonstrate command of the conventions of standard English capitalization, punctuation, and spelling when writing.

   a. Use punctuation (commas, parentheses, dashes) to set off nonrestrictive/parenthetical elements.*

Language: Knowledge of Language

L.6.3. Use knowledge of language and its conventions when writing, speaking, reading, or listening.

   a. Vary sentence patterns for meaning, reader/listener interest, and style.*

Common Core Standards, Grade 7

Language: Conventions of Standard English

L.7.1. Demonstrate command of the conventions of standard English grammar and usage when writing or speaking.

   a. Explain the function of phrases and clauses in general and their function in specific sentences.

   b. Choose among simple, compound, complex, and compound-complex sentences to signal differing relationships among ideas.

L.7.2. Demonstrate command of the conventions of standard English capitalization, punctuation, and spelling when writing.

Common Core Standards, Grade 8

Language: Conventions of Standard English

L.8.2. Demonstrate command of the conventions of standard English capitalization, punctuation, and spelling when writing.

   a. Use punctuation (comma, ellipsis, dash) to indicate a pause or break.

*Denotes standards requiring continued attention in higher grades

Student Activities Overview and Answer Key

Station 1

Students expand basic sentences written in present, past, and future tense by using a model provided.

Answers

Answers will vary. Accept any reasonable responses.

Station 2

Students identify simple, compound, and complex sentences in a newspaper article.

Answers

Answers will vary. Accept any reasonable responses.

Station 3

Students use three methods for correcting run-on sentences.

Answers

Depending upon the methods students choose for each run-on sentence, answers will vary. Accept all correct responses, but be sure that students have used each method in the chart at least once.

Station 4

Students determine whether or not sentences have parallel structure and explain their reasons.

Answers

1. NP; *swimming* does not use the same form as *to the mountains* and *to the beach*.

2. NP; *interviewed* and *write* do not use the same form.

3. NP; *to listen* and *talk* do not use the same form.

4. P; *under the sink* and *in the closet* are both prepositional phrases.

Materials List/Setup

Station 1   none

Station 2   one newspaper for each student (or any other grade-level reading); notebook paper

Station 3   none

Station 4   none

Discussion Guide

To support students in reflecting on the activities and to gather some formative information about student learning, use the following prompts to facilitate a class discussion to "debrief" the station activities.

Prompts/Questions

1. Name three parts of speech you can use to make a sentence more interesting. Provide supporting examples.

2. Explain the difference between compound and complex sentences.

3. Why is it important to avoid using run-on sentences?

4. What is parallel structure?

Think, Pair, Share

Have students jot down their own responses to questions, then discuss with a partner (who was not in their station group), and then discuss as a whole class.

Suggested Appropriate Responses

1. Adjectives, adverbs, and prepositional phrases can all be used to make sentences more interesting. Examples will vary.

2. A compound sentence is made up of two or more independent clauses, while a complex sentence is made up of one independent clause and at least one dependent clause.

3. Run-on sentences are difficult to read and understand.

4. Parallel structure means that related words or phrases in a sentence appear in the same grammatical form.

Possible Misunderstandings/Mistakes

- Confusing compound and complex sentences
- Not recognizing run-on sentences
- Not understanding that parallel structure needs to be consistent throughout a sentence

Language
Set 4: Sentences

Station 1: Improving Basic Sentences

A **simple sentence** tells one complete thought and has one complete subject and one complete predicate. But at the most basic level, a simple sentence can be boring to read. So, by adding descriptive words (adjectives and adverbs) and phrases (prepositional phrases), a writer can turn a basic sentence into one that grabs the reader's attention. Read the following examples.

> N – V model: The boy ran.
>
> Adj – N – V: The frightened boy ran.
>
> Adj – N – Adv – V: The frightened boy hurriedly ran.
>
> Adj – N – Adv – V – PP: The frightened boy hurriedly ran through the dark cemetery.

As you can see, each sentence gives more information and becomes more interesting.

Revise the following three basic sentences using the same model.

1. N – V model: The dog barked.

   a. Adj – N – V: _____

   b. Adj – N – Adv – V: _____

   c. Adj – N – Adv – V – PP: _____

   _____

2. N – V model: My dad works.

   a. Adj – N – V: _____

   b. Adj – N – Adv – V: _____

   c. Adj – N – Adv – V – PP: _____

   _____

3. N – V model: I will go.

   a. Adj – N – V: _____

   b. Adj – N – Adv – V: _____

   c. Adj – N – Adv – V – PP: _____

   _____

Share your answers with your group members. Discuss the different words different students chose to add to make the sentences more interesting. Which sentences are now most interesting?

Language
Set 4: Sentences

Station 2: Simple, Compound, and Complex Sentences

You will find a newspaper and notebook paper at this station. Use the newspaper to complete this station activity.

Read these definitions:

clause—a group of words that has a subject and an accompanying verb, and is used as a part of a sentence

independent clause—a group of words that expresses a complete thought and can stand alone as a sentence

dependent clause—a group of words that does not express a complete thought and cannot stand alone as a complete sentence

simple sentence—tells one complete thought, and has one complete subject and one complete predicate (The predicate is the verb plus any words that modify the verb.)
Example: The thief ran from the store. (The subject is "thief" and the predicate is "ran.")

compound sentence—made up of two or more independent clauses.
Example: The thief ran from the store; a DVD player was tucked under one arm.
("The thief ran from the store" and "a DVD player was tucked under one arm" would both be complete sentences if they were separated, so they are independent clauses.)

complex sentence—made up of one independent clause and at least one dependent clause.
Example: The thief, a young woman wearing a stocking cap, ran from the store with a DVD player tucked under her arm.
(The independent clause is "The thief ran from the store with a DVD player tucked under her arm," even though here it's divided by the dependent clause. The dependent clause is "a young woman wearing a stocking cap," because that phrase isn't a complete thought.)

Now follow these steps to complete the activity:

1. Choose one article from the newspaper.

2. Write the first five sentences of the article on a sheet of notebook paper. Number each sentence 1–5.

3. Decide if each sentence is simple (S), compound (C), or complex (CX).

4. Mark each sentence using the abbreviation shown in parentheses above.

Share your sentences with your group members. Be prepared to justify your answers.

Language
Set 4: Sentences

Station 3: Run-On Sentences

A **run-on sentence** is two or more sentences written together without any punctuation or joining words. Using run-on sentences is one of the most common mistakes writers make. This is a problem because run-on sentences are difficult to read and understand.

Read the following run-on sentence:

> Dan liked working on his motorcycle he thought that car mechanics were too hard for him.

This chart shows three ways to correct a run-on sentence.

Write the independent clauses as separate sentences.	*Dan liked working on his motorcycle. He thought that car mechanics were too hard for him.*
Use a semicolon to separate the independent clauses.	*Dan liked working on his motorcycle; he thought that car mechanics were too hard for him.*
Use a comma and a conjunction to separate the independent clauses.	*Dan liked working on his motorcycle, but he thought that car mechanics were too hard for him.*

Here are several run-on sentences that need to be corrected. Use a method from the chart above to correct each run-on sentence. Use each method at least one time.

1. The election is next month Mom and Dad are voting for different candidates.

   _____

   _____

2. It's been raining for 25 days straight the weatherman says there is no end in sight.

   _____

   _____

3. We went to see a movie to our surprise all the seats were sold out.

   _____

   _____

continued

Language
Set 4: Sentences

4. Lydia posts on her blog almost every day mostly she writes about things that happen at school.

_____

_____

5. The new television season isn't very interesting it seems as if there's nothing but reality shows.

_____

_____

6. I finished reading a book for class last night I was surprised that I really liked it.

_____

_____

Language
Set 4: Sentences

Station 4: Parallel Structure

Parallel structure means that related words or phrases in a sentence appear in the same grammatical form. Which one of these two sentences is correct?

   a. Rogelio enjoys playing board games and to read.

   b. Rogelio enjoys playing board games and reading.

The first sentence does not have parallel structure because the verbs *playing* and *to read* do not use the same form. The second sentence has parallel structure because the verbs *playing* and *reading* use the same form.

Which one of these two sentences is correct?

   c. I looked for the missing key under the table, on top of the refrigerator, and pockets.

   d. I looked for the missing key under the table, on top of the refrigerator, and in my pockets.

The first sentence does not have parallel structure because while *under the table* and *on top of the refrigerator* are prepositional phrases, *pockets* is not. The second sentence has parallel structure because *under the table, on top of the refrigerator*, and *in my pockets* are all prepositional phrases.

Read the following sentences. If the sentence is parallel, circle the *P* and explain your answer. If the sentence is not parallel, circle the *NP* and explain your answer.

  1. On our vacation we will go to the beach, to the mountains, and swimming. P NP

_____

_____

  2. When I worked for the school paper, I interviewed students and write stories. P NP

_____

_____

  3. I prefer to listen, not talk. P NP

_____

_____

  4. The paper towels are under the sink or in the closet. P NP

_____

_____

When you finish, discuss your answers with your group. Did you all agree?

Language

Set 5: Capitalization and Punctuation

Goal: To recognize and analyze different uses of capitalization and punctuation in a sentence

Common Core Standards, Grade 6

Language: Conventions of Standard English

L.6.2.   Demonstrate command of the conventions of standard English capitalization, punctuation, and spelling when writing.

    a. Use punctuation (commas, parentheses, dashes) to set off nonrestrictive/ parenthetical elements.*

Common Core Standards, Grade 7

Language: Conventions of Standard English

L.7.2.   Demonstrate command of the conventions of standard English capitalization, punctuation, and spelling when writing.

    a. Use a comma to separate coordinate adjectives (e.g., *It was a fascinating, enjoyable movie* but not *He wore an old[,] green shirt*).

Common Core Standards, Grade 8

Language: Conventions of Standard English

L.8.2.   Demonstrate command of the conventions of standard English capitalization, punctuation, and spelling when writing.

    a. Use punctuation (comma, ellipsis, dash) to indicate a pause or break.

Student Activities Overview and Answer Key
Station 1

Students identify the rules of capitalization that apply to a series of sentences.

Answers

1. a, c, e

2. a, b, d, e

3. a, c

4. a, d, e

5. a, b, d

Station 2

Students proofread a paragraph and correct capitalization errors.

*Denotes standards requiring continued attention in higher grades

Answers

See paragraph below. Corrections are underlined.

      How do members of your family share photos? <u>Not</u> that long ago, sharing photographs was a complicated process. You needed to have a <u>camera</u> and <u>film</u>. Once the pictures were taken, you sent the film to a developer, such as the <u>Kodak Company</u>. It might be a week before you could see your pictures and you still hadn't shared them! Nowadays, people use digital cameras and online sites such as <u>Flickr</u>. Within minutes, you can upload your pictures and e-mail <u>friends</u> and <u>family</u> to let them know that new pictures are posted.

Station 3

Students explain how adding commas changes the meaning of sentences.

Answers

Possible answers include the following:

1. In the first sentence, the man is crying over his lost tickets, but in the second sentence, the tickets are crying over the lost man.

2. In the first sentence, Elisa accuses Jason of stealing, and in the second sentence, Jason accuses Elisa of stealing.

3. In the first sentence, the speaker's dog calls the speaker's mother strange, but in the second sentence, the speaker's mother calls the dog strange.

4. The first sentence states that anyone who plays loud music at night should move. In the second sentence, the speaker is referring to specific people who happen to play loud music at night.

5. In the first sentence, the adjectives describe the color of Paulo's truck, but in the second sentence, the adjectives describe the weight and color of Paulo's truck.

Station 4

Students write a paragraph about a teacher-assigned topic, but do not use any punctuation. After trading papers, each student punctuates one of the student-written paragraphs.

Answers

Answers will vary. Accept any correct responses.

Materials List/Setup

Station 1	none
Station 2	none
Station 3	none
Station 4	a high-interest topic (chosen by the teacher); regular pencils and red pencils (one per student at the station)

Discussion Guide

To support students in reflecting on the activities and to gather some formative information about student learning, use the following prompts to facilitate a class discussion to "debrief" the station activities.

Prompts/Questions

1. Choose the rules of capitalization that are most confusing to you and explain why.

2. Discuss why proper capitalization is important.

3. How does comma use impact writing? Support your answer with an example.

4. Choose the punctuation mark you most need to learn more about and explain why.

Think, Pair, Share

Have students jot down their own responses to questions, then discuss with a partner (who was not in their station group), and then discuss as a whole class.

Suggested Appropriate Responses

1. Answers will vary, but the most likely responses will be the rules about proper nouns and capitalizing various titles.

2. Answers will vary, but should mention that readers often judge a writer by how well she or he has followed rules of grammar, including capitalization.

3. Improper use of commas can completely change the meaning of a sentence. Examples will vary.

4. Answers will vary.

Possible Misunderstandings/Mistakes

- Confusion about when to capitalize articles
- Confusion about whether or not to capitalize conjunctions that appear in titles of books, movies, etc.
- Overuse of commas

Language
Set 5: Capitalization and Punctuation

Station 1: Rules of Capitalization

Knowing when to capitalize words in a sentence is a skill that students practice beginning in kindergarten and continuing all the way through high school. In this station activity, you will match rules of capitalization to several sentences.

Here are five basic rules of capitalization:

    a. Capitalize the first word in a sentence.

    b. Capitalize the first word in a quotation if the quotation is a full sentence.

    c. Capitalize the words in the title of a book, a play, a song, a movie, a television show, and so on. Do not capitalize conjunctions, articles, and short prepositions unless they are the first word of a title.

    d. Always capitalize the pronoun *I*.

    e. Capitalize proper nouns and proper adjectives. This includes names of historical events, formal titles of documents, and titles before a person's name.

Each of the following sentences includes at least one example of proper use of capitalization. Read each sentence and, after the sentence, write the letter for each rule used.

Example: When does Mr. Lopez plan to grade our assignments? *a, e*

1. My favorite summer reading assignment was *Holes*, by Louis Sachar.

   _____

2. Mom's favorite saying is, "Don't count your chickens before they hatch," but I don't know what that means. _____

3. Have you ever seen *Finding Nemo*? _____

4. My dad is planning a family vacation to Orlando, Florida; I hope Disney World is on his list of things to do. _____

5. Rachel said, "I don't want to walk to school today." _____

Compare your answers with the answers of your group members. Be sure to discuss these questions:

- When do you capitalize a word such as *mom*, and when should it begin with a lowercase *m*?
- When is it proper to capitalize an article such as *the*?
- Is there ever a time when you do not capitalize the first word in a sentence or the pronoun *I*?

Language
Set 5: Capitalization and Punctuation

Station 2: Fixing Capitalization Errors

One of the most common mistakes proofreaders find is errors in capitalization. In this station activity, you will proofread a paragraph to find and correct capitalization errors. Remember, if a lowercase letter should be capitalized, draw three horizontal lines under the letter and write *cap* in the right margin. If a capitalized letter should be made lowercase, draw a vertical line (l) through that letter and write *lc* in the right margin.

Here are five basic rules of capitalization:

1. Capitalize the first word in a sentence.

2. Capitalize the first word in a quotation if the quotation is a full sentence.

3. Capitalize the words in the title of a book, a play, a song, a movie, a television show, and so on. Do not capitalize conjunctions, articles, and short prepositions unless they are the first word of a title.

4. Always capitalize the pronoun *I*.

5. Capitalize proper nouns and proper adjectives. This includes names of historical events, formal titles of documents, and titles before a person's name.

Find and correct the capitalization errors in the following paragraph.

How do members of your family share photos? not that long ago, sharing photographs was a complicated process. You needed to have a Camera and Film. Once the pictures were taken, you sent the film to a developer, such as the kodak company. It might be a week before you could see your pictures and you still hadn't shared them! Nowadays, people use digital cameras and online sites such as flickr. Within minutes, you can upload your pictures and e-mail Friends and Family to let them know that new pictures are posted.

Share your corrections with your group. Be prepared to justify your answers.

Station 3: Comma Chameleon

A comma is a punctuation mark that is used to separate words or groups of words in a sentence. Placement of a comma can change the entire meaning of a sentence. Consider the different meanings of these two sentences:

"Let's eat, Grandpa!"

"Let's eat Grandpa!"

How does adding or moving a comma change the meaning of the sentences in these examples? Without the comma, the second sentence suggests we should have Grandpa served up for lunch!

Read the sentence pairs below. Explain how adding or moving a comma changes the meaning of each.

1. a. His tickets lost, the man then cried.

    b. His tickets lost the man, then cried.

    _____

    _____

    _____

2. a. Elisa said Jason took the wallet.

    b. Elisa, said Jason, took the wallet.

    _____

    _____

    _____

3. a. My dog said my mother is strange.

    b. My dog, said my mother, is strange.

    _____

    _____

    _____

continued

4. a. I wish that those people who play loud music at night would move.

    b. I wish that those people, who play loud music at night, would move.

    _____

    _____

    _____

5. a. Paulo drives a light blue truck.

    b. Paulo drives a light, blue truck.

    _____

    _____

    _____

Share your answers with your group. Do other group members have different interpretations of the sentences? If so, what are the differences?

Language
Set 5: Capitalization and Punctuation

Station 4: Missing Punctuation

Your teacher will give you a topic for this station. You will find regular pencils and red pencils at this station. Use the pencils to complete this station activity.

Punctuation marks, such as periods and commas, are used to make the meaning of written work clear.

Using the regular pencil, write a paragraph about the topic your teacher assigns. <u>Do not use any punctuation marks in the paragraph.</u> However, think about different kinds of punctuation marks and try to write sentences in which several different marks can be used.

_____

_____

_____

_____

_____

_____

_____

_____

_____

_____

_____

_____

_____

Exchange papers with a group member. Now use a red pencil to correctly punctuate his or her paragraph.

When you are finished, return the paragraph back to your partner. Look at the punctuation marks she or he added. Do you agree with the punctuation used? Why, or why not? Discuss your thoughts with your partner.